Dreams of Flight

Also by Jena Woodhouse and published by Ginninderra Press
Farming Ghosts
As compiler-editor
Hidden Desires: Australian women writing, compiled and edited by
Christina Houen and Jena Woodhouse

Jena Woodhouse

Dreams of Flight

for Larisa and Romany

for H
for timely gifts of faith, hope and charity
διαλάμπει τὸ καλόν

and in memory of Anni S.,
through whom I first became aware
that we are part of others' stories,
as they are part of ours

Dreams of Flight
ISBN 978 1 74027 726 6
Copyright © text Jena Woodhouse 2014
Cover image: Lisa Adams (1969–) *1 Sparrow* 2009
oil on canvas
65.0 x 75.0 cm
Collection of The University of Queensland, purchased 2010. Reproduced courtesy the artist and Philip Bacon Galleries, Brisbane; photo Carl Warner
Photograph of author on back cover: Marcia McMenamin

First published in this form 2014
Reprinted 2020

GINNINDERRA PRESS
PO Box 3461 Port Adelaide 5015
www.ginninderrapress.com.au

Contents

Little Black Dress	9
The Agency of Water	14
An Uninvited Guest	23
Against the Current	30
The Gamblers	37
Stopover in Budapest	45
The Zeigarnik Effect	47
No Such Address	53
Horns of a Dilemma	58
The Tale of the Girl and the Tiger	63
Reading Rilke	66
Voices in the Wind	73
Love Me Tender	77
Fool's Gold	83
None But the Lonely Heart	87
Poor Blighter	97
The Agency of Love	102
Vergissmeinnicht	112
Billy Hunter	124
The Curlew's Cry	129
Hovering Over My Life	135
Acknowledgements	142

Fish leap for the stars,
possessed by dreams of flight.

I

Bird of Innocence

Little Black Dress

It was one of those increasingly rare occasions for us, a family gathering. Not the whole clan, which is pretty humungous. It was spur of the moment. My mum, my brothers and I decided to go and wish Mum's sister Nance a happy birthday. We didn't have any money for a present, but we've got used to not having money for stuff like that since Dad's been gone, so Mum simply got down to it and did her usual birthday thing: made a cake and some Anzac biscuits, and off we went.

We'd just demolished the cake, all gathered round in the kitchen with Aunt Nance's husband and kids, when we heard someone yoo-hooing through the living room, and who should appear in our midst but Aunt Mat.

Aunt Mat is something of a legend in our family. She travels a lot, so what we hear of her is often second-hand. She has this slightly mysterious, rather glamorous image, and I've heard her referred to as a dark horse, a black sheep, a lame duck, an *enfant terrible*, a bohemian, and a bit of a nomad. Depending on who was telling the story.

Anyway, the odd thing is, when you meet Matilda, she seems neither glamorous nor mysterious. She always looks as if her clothes were thrown together without much thought. On this occasion she was wearing a warm black top under a fluffy, sleeveless vest, but the other half of her outfit didn't match at all. The bottom half consisted of baggy old tracksuit pants, and, although it was winter, open sandals. Red hair (like mine), pale face, no make-up. That's my Aunt Mat.

She'd brought various bundles to distribute, another thing she's famous for. Birthday presents for Nance: two fluffy sleeveless vests like the one she was wearing herself, the price tags still attached. Various hand-me-downs, not very interesting. Mat's weight fluctuates, so she's always offloading things that are suddenly either too big or too small. But nobody ever looks good in her cast-offs. You need her kind of personality to get away with the outfits she wears, which are an original mixture of daring and daggy. (Half poodle, half blue heeler, Uncle Ted once rudely said.)

So I wasn't taking much notice, until she pulled out this scrunched-up black thing, gleaming here and there where it caught the light. She gave it a shake and held it up, and it fell into the shape of a dress, a little black party dress, very plain except where a border of shiny jet beads lured my gaze to the narrow, plunging neckline.

As soon as I saw it, I wanted it. That dress was made for me. I hoped Aunt Nance wouldn't put in a bid, seeing it was her birthday.

But Aunt Mat was looking at me as if something had just occurred to her. 'Here, Janey,' she was saying. 'I brought it for Nance, but you could wear this. I picked it up in Paris years ago, when I was young and slim.'

Out of the corner of my eye I saw Mum open her mouth as if to say something, and then think better of it and snap her lips shut like a coin purse. Everyone was looking at me. I was looking at Mat. Did she really mean it? She was holding the dress out for me to take. I looked at Mum for permission, but she gave no sign, just kept her lips tightly compressed. Nance didn't seem to want it either. She was into a more sporty look, you never saw her in slinky outfits.

I stretched out my fingers and touched the silky fabric. It felt almost alive. Mat sort of thrust it into my hand.

They were all still watching, and then Nance said, 'Aren't you going to try it on?'

I shook my head.

Someone fetched a carry bag, and the dress was bundled away out of sight, as if it was something scandalous or provocative. Then Nance and Mum made cups of tea and we took them out onto the deck.

Aunt Mat sidled up to me. 'I hope you enjoy the dress,' she said. 'It's been to many magical evenings: operas, parties, embassies, glamorous nights along the Seine, in Montparnasse… I'm glad it's yours now, Janey. Hope it brings you happiness. I always used to wear it to attract good luck.'

My head was on fire. Good luck in what, I wondered. True love? Success and fame? Mat had been unfortunate in both respects, they said. She had not been lucky in love and her career in art (she was a sculptor) had more downs than ups.

Very quietly I said, 'If Mum lets me wear it.'

Just at that moment, Mum, sniffing conspiracy, moved closer. 'You really shouldn't be giving Jane clothes that are far too old for her,' she reproached Mat.

Mat tried to be diplomatic. 'It's such an elegant little frock, Grace, don't you think? And young beauties like Janey, with her artist's-model hair, look stunning in simple black, trust me! It's the last word in chic and *savoir vivre*! You can't keep her rigged out like the von Trapps much longer. After all, she's turning seventeen this year, isn't she?'

Well, I doubted the dress would be going anywhere, at least on me. Perhaps I should mention here that my mum's a bit religious, although she's usually not too hard line about it. (Matilda, as far as we know, has no fixed religion.) Anyway, from the look in Mum's eye I could tell there was a sermon coming on, but fortunately Nance had spotted it too, so she stepped in and changed the subject.

When we got home I locked myself in my room, saying I had an important French assignment due on Monday. That was true. But first of all I took off all my clothes and slithered into the new satin camisole and knickers Nance had given me when I turned sixteen. I slipped the elastic band off my ponytail and took a long look at myself in the mirror. To my surprise, I liked what I saw – my smooth, creamy-white neck and shoulders, the satin clinging to my breasts reminded me of Aunt Mat's little clay maquettes of nymphs and dancers.

I slid the black dress out of the plastic bag, taking care not to make any loud rustling sounds, and slowly, very gently, lowered it over my head. It was a perfect fit.

I closed my eyes then opened them again. There was a hint of old, expensive perfume coming from the silk, and a faint but not unpleasant whiff of smoke. I fancied I could also sense traces of the musky scent of skin, of flesh, but it was so subtle, maybe I was imagining it. I closed my eyes again, and had the weird sensation of drinking in another world through the pores of my skin, as though someone's arms were enveloping me. I could feel my body moving in harmony with the other, the stranger's, a slow dance in a smoky room whose windows overlooked the Seine. I even fancied I could hear the murmur of voices, speaking French. I slowly circled in my room, dancing with eyes closed, synchronising my breathing with my imaginary partner's.

So at first I didn't hear Mum tapping at my door, not until she thumped it more insistently. 'Jane!' she was saying. 'Open up at once!'

Panicking, I twisted the key, grabbed the door handle and wrenched the door open so suddenly that she almost fell into the room. Bracing herself, she glared at me in frigid disapproval. Of course, the dress. I'd been so startled by her sudden knocking that I'd forgotten.

'What is the meaning of this?' she demanded. Then, in a quieter, more ominous tone, 'Take it off at once! I don't know what Matilda's thinking of, giving an innocent young girl clothes you'd see in a French film that no respectable person would watch! Look at the way it exposes your chest! It's indecent, not to mention unhealthy! What would Pastor Gander say?'

'Don't look at me then!' was all I could reply.

As soon as she turned her back, I dragged off the dress and grabbed my ordinary clothes.

She turned and snatched the little black dress, its beading flashing and glinting defiantly. 'I'll take that,' she said. 'I'll put it away where it won't give you the wrong kind of ideas.'

I knew it would be useless to protest. Perhaps that was the last I'd ever see of the tantalising garment. She'd bundle it into the bag of old clothes to donate to Lifeline. What she didn't know was that now, having seen myself in that dress, and danced the slow, romantic dance in a room above the Seine, with Matilda's lingering French perfume and the faintly masculine trace of smoke embracing me like ghosts in the fabric, nothing could ever be quite the same.

In those few minutes that I had worn it, the dress had become my dream passport. I didn't yet know where or when I'd be getting off the plane, but I did know that the little black dress would be there, in my luggage, one day.

The Agency of Water

Quatrefoil

♥ Stalking the Light

Her eyes open like clockwork. Five a.m. She swings her legs over the side of the bed, eyeing the uncurtained window. The water is already visible, reflecting the light from the sky.

Groping her way into tracksuit and joggers, she snatches up her camera and heads for the door, opening it quietly so as not to wake the children. Alert and expectant, her dog moves his rear from side to side in lieu of a phantom tail, but she never takes him on these morning forays. He would distract and slow her down.

She rushes past the houses between her own and the open stretch of river bank as if in hot pursuit of something, as indeed she is. If she misses the special effects of early-morning light on the river, her day will lack a meaningful beginning, and she'll have to wait until tomorrow for another opportunity. By sunrise it's already too late.

Hugging the river path like a stalker, she pauses at strategic points where there are spaces between the eucalypts on the bank or windows in the dense mangrove foliage below it, to focus her camera on the light refracted through clouds onto the water's surface then back again like a mirror through vapour, as if she could capture the radiance inside the small box housing the lens. To photo-graph means to write with light: a kind of alchemy. Her gaze searches the clouds and the water, tracking gaps and interstices, registering changes. These days she is always on the lookout for chinks and apertures, avenues for imagination to pursue, escape routes.

One year ago… No, it is to forget about one year ago that she is here, now, in the impressions of the moment, with the solitary canoeist whose craft draws a long chevron on the rose-tinted surface of the water below; with the cohort of ibis silhouetted against the forget-me-knot blue unveiled by dispersing cloud above; with the kingfishers and herons and magpies who frequent the early-morning river bank: here, now, in the strengthening light.

An hour later, the show is over. The sun has risen, soft shadows have fled like a flock of rose and grey galahs, and she has returned to her rented house, to the rented kitchen, to hear her own voice grating on silence, 'Hey, you lot! Get up! You'll be late for school.' Just as it had one year ago, two. Before she fled a hostile husband, security (or at least its semblance), and many other things she has since learned to live without.

Now she feels rich when she manages to catch the first light and carry home fleeting images of clouds, wings, waterbirds watching the sun inundate the river with running fire; rays glancing off spider webs; tiny glazed beads, seed on grass heads; weeds unfurling delicate flowers only she seems to notice; the minute detail of dead and living trees: boundless gifts revealed to her by first, fresh, pristine light.

In the house she has leased near the river, her photographs occupy every wall: nuanced images captured on film in her dawn sorties. Her former house, hemmed in by leafy suburban avenues, was equally crowded with reproductions of French Impressionist paintings. Living there, she'd had no inkling of what the future held, no awareness of the river meandering only a short walk away. Nor did she rise so early.

Now she rises at five a.m. without an alarm – her body knows, and responds along with the plants and all living creatures to the shift in energies triggered by the transition from darkness to light, from nycthemeral rhythms to circadian ones.

Now, with the sinuous ribbon of water gliding past the bottom of her garden, mornings are the magic in her day. Other people who exercise along this reach never carry cameras, never seem to pause, to stand and gaze more intently. It seems to be her private discovery.

Another morning, another revelation. The same river, yet always different. And oh look! Hot-air balloons, rising like a vision from another world, somewhere beyond the mangroves fringing the opposite bank – ascending effortlessly, soundlessly, not brightly coloured, but in muted shades of grey. And below them, her fellow traveller of the morning, the lone canoe and its occupant. Feverishly she records them before they move out of frame – the balloons, the river, the canoeist, the light's mounting intensity. It is the most satisfying concatenation of images in a year of mornings.

She has a disquieting premonition that even these pleasures are about to be taken from her. Without knowing that the next day her son will drop and break her camera. Without knowing that her capricious landlord is about to play one of his habitual power games and not renew her lease.

Meanwhile, here, now, the morning suffuses her with its lustre, so that as she turns homeward, it is as if the renewed energy inside her is becoming radiant, as energy does when a new star forms. It is as if she is floating above the treetops, powered invisibly yet palpably by helium, which is also converting into inner light; looking down on the river as it wells with gold; looking east to the lava flow on the horizon; looking up at the innocent blue vault of the expanding sky, before glancing briefly, just once, back at herself in her former life, which appears so small, so diminished by distance, that it is barely discernible.

For L.M.B.

Cara

I was running late for the concert, driving recklessly through early spring rain then dashing headlong from Hope Street to the concert hall just as the doors were closing. I'd been looking forward to this performance of the Vaughan Williams Symphony No. 1, *A Sea Symphony*. Luckily I already had my ticket. A disapproving, ageing usherette admitted me. Grudgingly. I wondered why the young man I had to pass to reach my seat did not retract his feet as I edged past, until the young woman beside him murmured, 'Mind the dog.'

A black Labrador lay at the feet of another young man in the seat next to mine. Both youths were stylishly attired in what looked like Italian tailoring, which complemented their classical features and dark good looks. Fleetingly their bearing evoked memories of sculpture – the beautiful ephebe beloved of Greece and Rome. Between the two youths sat two girls of similar age. The one who had warned me about the dog appeared to have no visual impairment; the other was so finely boned, so fair, so delicate, it seemed that she might wither under stronger light. Her outfit was a feminine version of those the young men wore. A fine gold chain adorned her throat and she wore tinted glasses.

Throughout the first part of the programme – Schumann's Piano Concerto in A minor Op. 54 the *Phantasie* – I found my attention divided between the musicians and the young concertgoers in the adjacent seats, who, listening intently with an air of composure and unselfconscious vulnerability, seemed to be experiencing the music from a place apart, which I could neither imagine nor enter.

During the intermission, the usherette distributed publicity material. She handed a small booklet to the girl wearing tinted lenses, who turned it this way and that in her hands, registering it as an object without attempting to read it. The young man next to me commented on the odour of damp dog. I asked the dog's name.

'Cara,' he said.

'That means "black" in Turkish,' I said, proffering one of those random snippets of information one garners in the course of one's travels.

He leaned towards the other young man and relayed this detail.

They both seemed amused and said, almost in the same breath: 'It suits her. She's a black dog.'

Then the one sitting next to me added, 'But in Italian, her name means "dear".'

I asked his permission to pat Cara.

'It's okay. She's off duty now,' he said.

Cara didn't mind me stroking her, but I was wishing that all the people from the opposite end of the row would not insist on exiting from our end and returning past us, stepping over Cara, who looked uneasy but sat quietly. I was already feeling protective of her and her charges, the young man next to me and his ethereal-looking companion, who inclined their torsos towards each other, fingers interlaced, cocooned in the same aura.

I thought of sculpture in the rain, marble streaked with centuries of spring showers, human forms of purity and beauty, eloquent in their sightlessness, sequestered in some forgotten Mediterranean courtyard wreathed in wind-tossed jasmine. In that rain-rinsed garden one could perhaps catch a glimpse of the Bird of Innocence – a shy, legendary creature in flight from the shop-soiled world, whose song was for the pellucid of spirit.

The second half of the programme commenced: *A Sea Symphony*. The chorale and soloists delivered Whitman's lyrics. All around us surged the tide, augmented by the gale and tempest unleashed by the orchestra. Grandeur and majesty. Intonations of an age that still believed in certainties. Beneath the surface textures of sound, the cadences and frequencies and energies of symphony. Stealing a glance at the faces of the youth and girl beside me, I perceived, in their rapt expressions, that they were immersed in a private realm whose structure was defined by sound; its architecture – music. Innocent of their own beauty, they could not have been aware of how they appeared to the eyes of their unknown observer, to whom their world seemed perfect and complete.

At the end of the concert, with tempestuous sound waves vibrating into silence, the lights came on, Cara's keeper snapped the hand-grip onto her harness, and she rose eagerly and began to strain towards the exit, wagging her tail in anticipation. 'Let's go!' her body language said. 'Let's go home!'

Arm in arm, the lily-pale girl and her slender, dark-haired companion exited with Cara and their two friends. They were a family, a closed circle.

Unaccountably forlorn, I remained seated and watched them leave, wishing they might sense me there, wanting to farewell them as one does close friends, but knowing I was unlikely ever to see them again. A voice in me was whispering, 'Take me with you, into that serenity you emanate…'

What is it that sighted people miss? I have been wondering ever since. If I were to trade places with the young concertgoers for a time, might I learn to read the world more clearly by my inner light? If the power to restore their sight were granted, would Cara's family see a different world from the one their other senses have constructed? And would they perhaps wonder at the kinds of blindness that sometimes afflict the sighted as well?

🐬 Dolphin

Why is Belinda, a girl not grown into her bones, never home for dinner these days? Flora can't swallow her daughter's story about a school project, but how else is she to account for Belinda's absence? And since when did girls still in primary school come home from working on a project with paint on their lips and eyelids? How did Belinda come by such things? Flora knows that if she were to ask, she'd be served up a big fat lie. Belinda is concealing something from her mother. Flora is hiding something from herself.

Down at the docks, the flash of hair ornaments and cut-glass earrings flag the spot where Belinda and her new friends wait near the shipping containers. Nervous giggles and muffled exchanges suddenly cease as a lighter approaches. A mooring rope lassos a bollard. Belinda's companions push her forward.

'Get in!' the boatman tells her tersely.

They head out across the murky water to where the freighters are moored: unseaworthy hulks that nonetheless ply between east Asia and this Pacific archipelago, taking on timber, ore and tuna. The incidental catch of smaller fish, prized by the locals, can be had only in exchange for a 'dolphin', a pubescent girl. No dolphin, no fish: simple as that.

The police turn a blind eye, claiming it would be impossible to catch the offenders in the act, as they would notice the launch approaching.

Tonight, Belinda is to be the dolphin.

Her friends have groomed her for the event, told her what to expect. 'They give you fizzy drink, you feel good. After, you wake up, go home. Boatman gives you pocket money, nice clothes, earrings.'

Belinda can sense the air of importance this secret thing has conferred on her friends, but she feels only spasms of foreboding in her belly as the lighter approaches the ship's black bulk. Above, men's voices are speaking a language she can't understand.

'I want to go home!' a small, childish voice blurts out. Was it her own?

The boatman ignores her, then jerks his head towards a rope ladder dangling within reach. 'Go!' he says.

Belinda is trembling so violently that she doesn't think she'll be able to grasp the rope with her hands, or steady her knees. 'I want to go home,' wails a voice in her head, but this time she doesn't say it aloud.

It is after midnight when the lighter returns to port. A small, dishevelled figure is huddled aft, surrounded by baskets of fish, their eyes gaping starward. Nauseous, Belinda retches over the side as they approach the mooring. Where are her friends now?

The boatman bundles her roughly ashore. 'Go home,' he mutters, half to himself, thrusting a few coins into her hand.

Her skirt feels sticky. She touches it with the fingers of her other hand, then holds them up to the dingy light. Blood.

A woman steps from the shadows, but Belinda is too dazed to notice. Her knees buckle. She wants to lie down. Weep. Sleep.

'Belinda!' says a peremptory voice. An arm slips under her shoulders, across her back, supporting her.

She leans against the cotton print smock that smells of laundry soap and they set off, slowly, heavily, for home.

Her mother gives her a little shake, rough but not threatening. 'Wake up!' she says. 'Wake up, child, before it's too late!'

There is no response from Belinda.

'Is this how you want to live?' Flora demands.

In the indigo dusk, Flora senses an almost imperceptible movement at her breast as her daughter weakly shakes her head.

🍂 Death by Water

There is a dream I have which comes in many forms. Its common element is water, not in the guise of life-giver but as marauding force, a tide that rises swiftly and inexorably, engulfing human artefacts and structures. I live in a city built along a water artery whose river sometimes floods, although floodwaters have never threatened me. Perhaps the dream is a subliminal effect of the river's presence: its magnetic currents coursing past my house and travelling unimpeded through my sleep, relaying messages.

The morning after experiencing another version of this dream, I learn that a boy from the international college where I teach has drowned. He was thrown into the river late the previous evening, during a thunderstorm, by several classmates. All the boys are from Asian countries. They have been playing this dangerous game night after night for several weeks. None of them is a confident swimmer, but this boy could not swim at all. The culprits, his former classmates, insist that he was laughing when they threw him in, that when he failed to surface, they dived in to search for him, but the current snatched him out of their hands. Police divers are continuing the search. What is the psychological truth beneath the surface of these events?

In the afternoon of the following day, the drowned boy is found near the ferry pontoon. His shoelace was caught on a submerged shopping trolley, so there had been no chance of his floating free in time to save himself. His classmates will eventually stand trial for manslaughter. His parents will be childless from now on.

That night it rains again. At the deserted, brightly illumined college, a couple of figures shelter, silhouetted at the top of the steps in the lights from the foyer, waiting for the rain to ease before making their way home.

As I drive through the gentle, persistent rain, I think of strangers all over the city, separated from one another by crystal chains of water droplets, and of the drowned boy, lying now in shrouds of dry, cold darkness, as his parents fly above the clouds from another land to reclaim their son.

I think of the people in high white hospital beds, lying in brightly lit wards, lonely for their homes and their families, wistfully waiting for health to return, aware or unaware of the rain that brings some closer and separates others.

I think of the time I was thrown into a deep waterhole by classmates who derided my ineptitude at all games requiring physical prowess. I remember how they rolled on the bank, laughing uproariously as I surfaced gasping and choking, and sank, several times. (Did the drowned boy's friends laugh when he panicked?) To that experience I owe my terror of water when out of my depth. Although I can swim, panic rises in me as soon as my feet can no longer touch bottom. The thought of the drowned boy's ordeal fills me with personal, palpable horror.

I also remember Synge's play *Riders to the Sea*, the drowned Aran fishermen who seemed to live under the curse of some cruel pelagic law of sacrifice: the almost ritualistic nature of their deaths; the lives of their mothers, sisters, children and wives stretched on the tenterhooks of perpetual mourning.

And as it rains from sombre skies for a third night, it is as if some metaphysical clepsydra of sorrow is being replenished, as part of a cycle of catharsis only dimly sensed, when we brush up against it in the darkness from time to time.

An Uninvited Guest

Although it had become known as 'the Swedish house', the only Swedish thing about it was its owner, Torvald Tolmersson, a man his neighbours seldom caught a glimpse of. However, while its architect and builder had been local people with no Swedish connections, the house had a distinctly Nordic feel, being a structure of timber and glass permeated by light from the river, more reminiscent of a floating craft than a sedentary dwelling.

The facade, curved in an arc like a bow, enhanced the impression of a boat poised on a grassy embankment above the waterline. It was the kind of house that would have looked equally at home in a Scandinavian pine wood or on the set of a Chekhov play; a modest dacha such as a moderately successful writer or painter might aspire to own. Somehow those who had designed and built the house three-quarters of a century earlier had captured the nuances of a vernacular with which they were unlikely to have had any familiarity.

It was not surprising that the house overlooking the river at its widest, wildest point, facing the mangrove fringes and eucalypts of the deserted opposite bank, had struck a responsive chord in Torvald Tolmersson. It had simply been love at first sight, catching him unawares with flashbacks to childhood summers at his grandparents' cottage in Helsingland. He arranged to buy the house within an hour of sighting it, without even stopping to consult his wife, Mai Song, whom he had met on his travels through East Asia and regarded as the love of his life.

This was an unfortunate omission, for the aversion Mai Song felt for the house on first sight was as intense as her husband's instant attraction had been. Not that she expressed her reaction initially, for she was not contentious by nature and hoped her first impression would not last.

So it was that Torvald Tolmersson, flushed with the pride of the successful purchaser, ensconced himself and his bride of a year in the house by the river. As the weeks passed, he began to feel more and more at home in his timber and glass light trap over-looking the water. He had inherited sufficient money not to need to work on a regular basis, but nonetheless liked to keep himself busy with the occasional contract in his métier as a sound engineer, and occupied himself at home constructing model fishing boats and yachts, alternating with maintenance tasks on the old house and neglected yard. Naturally, he assumed that Mai Song shared his sense of well-being in their new dwelling. For in his glow of satisfaction, it took Torvald some time to notice the change in his wife's demeanour, until one afternoon when she scorched a batch of apple muffins and burst into prolonged and uncontrollable sobbing. It occurred to him then that perhaps there was more than scorched muffins upsetting her, though he had no idea what. At this point another detail came into focus: her silences during their morning and evening walks by the river. He recalled that she had been chirpy as a wren until they moved to the riverside.

At first Mai Song seemed reluctant to tell him what was bothering her. She could see how much her husband loved the house, and had no wish to mar his pleasure in it. Nevertheless, his persistent attempts to elicit a reason for her silences and hysterical outburst wore down her defences, whereupon he was astonished to learn the truth.

'This house!' she burst out. 'I do not like this house! I do not want to live here!'

Torvald could scarcely believe his ears. 'But what is wrong with it, Mai Song?' he asked. 'I know it's not a new house, but look where it is! There's no more beautiful place for a house anywhere along this river…'

'Wrong feng shui!' said Mai Song emphatically. 'Right for you, wrong for me. And also, the river should be at the front door, not the back door.'

'I don't understand,' he protested. 'What's wrong with the river being where it is?'

Mai Song would not explain, other than to say, 'This is something I feel and I know.'

Torvald was thrown into consternation by his wife's words. He was by now almost as much in love with his house as he was with her. He was happy there, and had somehow assumed that she must be, too. Now his awareness that this was not the case made him more observant, and he could no longer fail to notice that her mechanical movements and responses belied her former pretence that all was well.

Torvald, laconic by nature, was nonplussed. It was difficult for him to ask Mai Song for guidance, but that was what he would have to do.

'Mai Song, would you like us to live somewhere else?' he blurted out one morning. As usual, they were taking coffee under a tulip tree on the embankment overlooking the river.

Although her face brightened at the prospect, she took her time to respond. 'What about you?' she said. 'You like it here. I think you will not be so happy somewhere else.'

If he had been hoping her attitude to the house might have softened, now he could tell that it hadn't. He sighed a sorrowful inward sigh, but already knew what he must do. Neither of them said anything further on the subject, drinking their coffee in silence.

Mai Song was an artisan who worked in fabric, creating wall hangings and other decorative pieces from silk and traditional textiles. Her creative energy had languished of late, and she sometimes sat idly in her workshop at one end of the arced facade, staring out at the front garden, not motivated to work as she had been in the past. She seemed to avoid even looking at the river, while Torvald craved the proximity of water. Imperceptibly, yet seemingly inexorably, the river had come between them, insinuating its presence as a divisive force, strangely inaudible yet pervasive.

Whereas Torvald's first impression had been of the glistening stream cradling the house in the crook of its arm, Mai Song sensed only the threat of the river's encroachment: a trap. She had seen this happen before, long ago, and had never forgotten. The river could metamorphose to a crocodile and drag the house under, drowning it then devouring it.

Torvald was not to know that Mai Song's family had lived by a flood-prone river when she was very young, and she was not about to tell him, since she had resolved to suppress her qualms for her husband's sake.

She remembered the time when that other river had inundated her village and they lost their home, and many people drowned, or disappeared forever. She had been almost too young to understand, but the terror she had witnessed never faded. She remembered her parents searching and calling for her missing brother, the weeping and lamentation, the cries for help as the waters receded. She had wished never to live near a river again, and until now that wish had been granted. When they moved into the house by the river, the horror of the flood returned with such force that she had had difficulty concealing it from Torvald.

Several weeks passed, until one day Torvald arrived home after a few hours' absence and said, 'Come, Mai Song, I have something to show you.'

He drove her only as far as a street in a neighbouring suburb, and led her through a gate in a high white wall to a modern house in a cubist style, its internal courtyard landscaped in a way reminiscent of Japanese Zen gardens with rocks, pebbles and a few dwarf trees. Mai Song could imagine her works in silk on the walls of this house. She had declined to hang them in the other house among the model boats. They did not belong there. Here it would be different.

'If you like it,' said Torvald, 'we can buy it.' He could tell from the look in her eyes that this was what she wanted.

Mai Song was as happy in the new house as Torvald had been in the old one. Now it was his turn to feel unaccountably out of place. He was partly consoled by the thought that he had kept the house by the river. Since he still owned it, he could dream of one day living there again. In the meantime, he would let it to a suitable tenant.

The tenant who signed the lease was a musician and piano teacher, a woman in her early forties, a few years younger than Torvald. Her grand piano occupied the large central room at the back of the house, with a glass wall facing the water, and her music would ripple out across the river morning and evening, much to Torvald's delight on the occasions when he happened to be passing, checking that his house was still safe. He caught himself imagining what it might be like to live in this house, with that woman, but instantly felt twinges of disloyalty to Mai Song.

As the house was under agency management, the tenant had not met her landlord, so when Torvald appeared unannounced with a ladder and toolkit she let him in, assuming he was a tradesman, come as requested to replace some light fittings. He eavesdropped on a piano lesson like a jealous lover, and only as he was leaving did he gruffly introduce himself.

After that meeting, he found himself remembering her dark eyes, her elegant wrists and hands framed by the little ruffs of fur trimming her cardigan sleeves; the strong, slender fingers with shell-pink, unvarnished nails. She wore a baroque pearl ring on one of her fingers, but no other jewellery. He had noticed her graceful neck exposed by upswept dark hair. Involuntarily, he began to fantasise that the woman who made music flow from his house on the river was his clandestine mistress.

Being of a phlegmatic disposition, he was taken aback by these wayward fancies. Yet they persisted. Knowing the house intimately, he could imagine himself in it with her and her piano. Even when a lover eventually moved in to share the house with her, Torvald could not stop himself imagining that *he* was in fact the one who lived there, as indeed part of him still did. But the lover apparently never took to the place and left after a few months.

The torrents of notes continued unabated. Torvald continued to turn up with his ladder and toolkit whenever something needed fixing, though sometimes the pretext was a flimsy one. The pianist was pleased to have such a considerate landlord. She liked his attention to detail. And she adored the house, as she assured him on each encounter. She so hoped it would not be sold. She couldn't understand why the rent was so low, but of course this was not a thought she ever voiced to the owner or agent.

Every month without fail, the agent asked the landlord the same questions:

– Do you want to sell?

– Do you want to renovate?

– Do you want to raise the rent?

The response to all three questions was invariably a curt 'No'.

As for Mai Song, Torvald could not fail to notice her contentment in her new surroundings. She radiated well-being, and was attentive to his comfort as never before. He was neither unmindful nor ungrateful. She was still the flesh and blood woman he desired, while the pianist inspired an unattainable, parallel fantasy life.

On nights when Torvald was aroused by Mai Song's nearness and her welcoming warmth, he would momentarily forget the disjunction that troubled him like chafed skin: he had both the woman he desired and the house of his dreams. It was just unfortunate that he couldn't enjoy both at the same time, in the same place.

To add to his perplexity, only the previous day the pianist had turned the mesmeric force of her gaze full on his startled eyes and asked him if he'd like her to play for him one evening, an invitation he accepted as impulsively as he had purchased the house.

*

Six months after that invitation, there were unprecedented deluges in the river's catchment area. Cars were swept off roads by flash floods, their drivers and passengers drowned. Houses in the path of the torrents collapsed like cardboard cartons. Their occupants' remains were found kilometres away, or never found. The devastation in some outlying communities was beyond imagining.

Downstream, the waters swelled and rose, swirling towards the Swedish house, a sinister and uninvited guest. Breaching the bank in a tongue-like surge, the leading edge advanced, swarming up the slope towards the house like the forward scouts of an invasion force. Torvald arrived in time to see the grand piano being loaded into a removal van, but the distraught pianist lost many of her treasured trinkets and personal effects to the turbid waters. With the greed of an indiscriminate predator, the river snatched crystal ornaments and delicate items of apparel, leaving its signature of foul-smelling, viscid mud.

Torvald was speechless. His dream house was defiled, and with it his fantasy world with the alluring tenant, which, like the river's rising waters, had gradually crept up on, and threatened to inundate, his harmonious life with his wife.

Only Mai Song seemed unperturbed, as if she had sensed all along that it would come to this, and was now vindicated.

Against the Current

We were all watching her that day. It's what she liked. She liked to be the centre of attention. It was a game of fox and hounds, with us sometimes playing the fox, sometimes the hounds. We were usually rewarded for our vigilance by her faux pas, and having once put a foot wrong, she had a disconcerting tendency to go off at a tangent to the rest of the company, as if to throw the hounds off the scent. As if we didn't know!

They were all watching me that day. It wasn't what I wanted. I wanted to become invisible. But since they had nothing better to do, I quickly decided that it was game on.

We wives raised our eyebrows and our hostess rolled her eyes when Lucinda arrived without Steven. Her husband is our colleague, yet she had come alone. Presumably poor Steven was assigned to babysitting duties. It wouldn't be the first time. When she walked into the room where we were waiting before boarding the launch, she seemed to realise she'd made a gaffe. It was a full half-minute before she remembered to say good morning.

I didn't realise until Steven stopped the car outside the house with the jetty that he'd really wanted to come after all. At least, he intimated as much to the owner of the launch. So I felt foolish when I went upstairs and met a battery of raised eyebrows and pursed lips. I could almost hear them thinking, 'She's done it again!' Why was I there anyway? I didn't like Steven's colleagues, and they didn't like me. Then I remembered that it was because of the island. We were going down the river on a private launch to visit a small island, more like an islet, in fact, that had been, until recently, a lazaret – a place to quarantine people with leprosy. Now that history had been eclipsed by tourism, the uninhabited islet, one of many fanning out across the bay like the eyes in a peacock's tail, was simply a destination for day trips. But it was precisely because of its history that I wanted to visit that place, and the only way you could get to it was by private boat. Admittedly, my motive was not entirely rational. I believed that once I had been to the island, I'd understand why I needed to go there. While I have always been drawn to the liminal, I was aware that the terms of existence imposed on sufferers of Hansen's disease had been more of the order of stigmatisation and exclusion. So for me this was to be no mere jaunt.

While I was glancing from face to face in confusion, hoping to encounter a glimmer of goodwill, a curious by-play occurred. McPhee, the newest staff member, was standing apart from the others, near a window, against the soft grey background of a cloudy day, mimicking my movements. When I gave an involuntary shrug, more like a shudder, I saw him mirror it. I was so startled I forgot to greet them, then I realised they were all still watching me. For several seconds I floundered, at a loss for words.

We wondered what she was up to this time. What did she see in the prospect of a boat trip down the river? We tacitly decided to keep an eye on her. Wherever she cropped up, unaccountable things happened.

It was a perfect setting for the transmutations that ensued – an April day of atmospheric grace and quiet lucidity: a delicate and flawless aquarelle; the clouds soft, voluminous as eiderdowns. The light that filtered through was muted, yet marvellously clear, the limpid water a translucent grey. Against this diaphanous backdrop, the islet, with its grim history, loomed in my consciousness as a stab of foreboding: an entrance to Hades, where the earth waited to swallow the afflicted. A place of no return, thronged with the shades of those who had been forbidden to leave. While the prospect of setting foot there filled me with trepidation – the intimation of a lingering, disfiguring death – it was only by crossing that imagined threshold that the sense of dread could perhaps be allayed.

The journey down the river took a long time. We passed beneath the breathtaking new bridge. Above our heads, the two unfinished halves were almost touching. At first, Lucinda had quite a lot to say and as usual she talked about herself. Our professor's wife cut her down to size on one occasion. It seems that Lucinda had organised a student function, but the professor's wife made it sound as if all the credit was due to someone else. You have to remind opinionated people of their place, and our professor's wife is very good at that. Whereupon Lucinda seemed to shrink into herself. We assumed she was sulking.

I wanted to envelop myself in an imaginary protective membrane, become translucent as a medusa and slip away, out of range of baited words and barbed glances. Or, even more impracticably, to become airborne, elusive as plumed seeds blown from a dandelion or thistle. But I was no ethereal being. I was just an uninvited guest, as I'd realised belatedly, who, in my perverse desire to reach the islet of the damned, had blundered into a social impasse by embarking on a long day's journey as the odd one out in a company that clearly regarded me as an interloper.

As for Steven's lot in life, we all knew he was making a mistake in marrying Lucinda (a twee sort of name, as Klinghoffer remarked). She's totally disastrous in the role of wife to an up and coming academic. For all the world like something out of Chekhov, gone wrong. In company, she invariably manages to strike the wrong note and then remain offkey: either too sharp or too flat. She's one of those irritating people who are always onto something (or someone) new and has to let the whole world know. At the moment it's vegetarianism and Sufi dancing, though who would venture to predict what next week will bring? But then, Steven *had* intimated on several occasions that she could be unstable, which was all the more reason not to indulge her childish caprices.

The journey down the river was fairly uneventful. I got the usual rap across the knuckles from Madame (senior academics' wives do tend to put on airs), but mostly I was contemplating the light, the way the sea and sky refracted it through one another, like mirrors faintly clouded by warm breath, so that everything shimmered with a muted pearly lustre. As we moved towards the river mouth, we could see ships waiting to come into port, and they seemed to be moored up in the sky, floating in the air between the clouds and water. At first I was rather nervous and overexcited, trying to register the attitudes of the people Steven worked with. A couple of the women seemed quite friendly. McPhee had donned his mask of old Oxonian sangfroid.

Eventually I was soothed by the dreamlike gliding of the launch, the lucent mutability of light and water. Yet the stark, unfinished arcs of the new bridge somehow disturbed me. The chasm where they failed to meet seemed to defy geometry. I thought of hands that strained towards each other but could never touch. Involuntarily, my glance strayed to McPhee, but I quickly averted my gaze before anyone could notice.

*

Having decided to give the former leper colony a miss, we moored near the mouth of the river, the weather out on the bay being too uncertain, our skipper said. Besides, none of us had any great desire to visit such an obscure island – probably just a glorified mudbank, in those shark-infested waters. Anyway, most of us (all except one, in fact) had brought delicious food, and our hostess kept us plied with wine, so we could see no reason not to stay on board and lunch at our leisure. Our professor's daughter did a spot of fishing. We all rushed aft whenever she caught something, but were disappointed that she landed nothing we could eat.

I was sitting gazing out over the stern when Rosemary started to fish. I hoped she wouldn't catch any, but nevertheless I felt a perverse thrill when she managed to land a few small fry, exquisite as slivers of moon, most likely whiting or perch, silver as a wish. My momentary pleasure was extinguished by the sight of the hook piercing the delicate jaw. McPhee was hovering around, and each time Rosemary drew another fishlet from the water, he would gently extricate the hook and release the quivering creature overboard. I was surprised to see him handling the fish without any hesitation. At the welcome party held in his honour, I'd heard him express repugnance for batrachia in particular – as he termed green tree frogs and the like – and local fauna in general. Perhaps the talk I'd overheard was merely for effect.

Behind me I could hear and smell the signals that meant food. I didn't go to help the busy ladies quacking in the galley. The cabin was small, I'd brought only apples, because Steven hadn't mentioned one was expected to bring picnic fare, and anyway I could not contribute to exclamations over the rich viandes – roast duck, pâté and the like. Still, they would not let me exclude myself completely.

They enjoyed their repast for what seemed an eternity of lip-smacking and commentary on the qualities of the food. They obligingly passed me salad through the hatch. The wine was going to my head.

Lucinda managed to stay aloof from the meal, just as she'd avoided contributing to it. Was it holier than thou, some of us wondered. You know how it is with vegetarians. One of the party had a little dig at her about it while we were having coffee, and she flew at him in no uncertain terms. Then quite artlessly he happened to mention a friend with a flock of geese that would make good eating, and asked her if she'd ever tasted roast goose. We all licked our lips at the thought. All except her, that is. She informed him haughtily that she'd had roast goose for Christmas as a child, but now knew better. She now believed, along with the ancient Japanese, that a white goose was a symbol of the soul. Then she confused us utterly with some Hindu-sounding mumbo-jumbo about the next incarnation. Perhaps, she speculated with her typical effrontery, we (herself presumably excluded) would come back as geese, at the mercy of somebody like our colleague. Trust her to leave a nasty taste in everyone's mouth!

The meal was finally over. The other women went into a gaggle of activity over soggy tea towels. The launch seemed very small. It was impossible to isolate myself. I could sense eyes trained on me at times through the portholes of the cabin, and there was always someone else on deck, a few feet away. The wife of the man whose friend kept geese struck up a conversation, and I started to tell her about the Whirling Dervishes and their ecstatic dance, when the hostess's voice suddenly cut in via the galley hatch, sounding as acid as her words. 'You should have done all that when you were young!'

On the way back we noticed the professor saying something to her, but the only person near enough to catch it was Klinghoffer's wife. Intriguing. You could see Madame was not amused.

Since the weather was uncertain, we couldn't approach the site of the former lazaret. By this time, claustrophobic though I felt confined to the small deck, uncomfortably aware of McPhee's enigmatic scrutiny, I was preoccupied less with the destination than the unforeseen complexities of the journey.

On the way back, glistening filaments of rain moved in the air like a spinnaker, or the sheerest of parachutes billowing over the bay. The flimsy strands became heavier, denser, opaque as muslin, gathering in towards the launch like draperies screening a four-poster bed, the vessel's gentle rocking reminiscent of the transitions of dream. I love the interplay of sea and rain. Water is the element of melancholy.

Adrift in my own reverie and nebulous sensations, I was startled when a voice reverberated in my ear. The voice was saying something about poverty... Manila... I couldn't think of anything to say. I'm not familiar with that kind of poverty. I don't think the professor is, either.

We noticed young McPhee hovering around her too. Someone ought to warn him she can be slippery as an eel. But we kept an eye on things that day. He was quite safe with us there. Once he leaned towards her and said something, and she looked surprised, then wistful. Klinghoffer's wife, who was close enough to eavesdrop, or at least read their lips, will no doubt regale us with the details.

Having committed the initial faux pas of joining our cruise without her husband, Lucinda had – deservedly, it must be said – found herself increasingly on the outer. It seems to take some people a long time to learn their place.

*

We were drifting deeper into grey, where the only colours were the scattered mooring lights.

McPhee, who'd been sitting opposite, studying me, leaned forward. 'You look like the little mermaid in Copenhagen.'

I pretended to shrug off the comment – or was it a compliment? What had prompted the observation, and why did I feel so utterly disarmed by it?

Like the little mermaid of Andersen's tale, I was indeed out of my element in that uncongenial company, and feeling increasingly crestfallen at the realisation that Steven's colleagues would always look at me askance.

*

Sometimes there is a longing for trajectories that seem not to end. There is romance in the texture of rain against glass, casting patterned shadows like a coarse-grained veil on faces moving swiftly under street lamps, congealing into scatterings of brilliants; pausing in its coursings inexplicably, inarticulate and blind as tears.

The Gamblers

> One moment in Annihilation's Waste,
> One moment of the Well of Life to taste –
> The Stars are setting, and the Caravan
> Starts for the dawn of Nothing – Oh, make haste!
>
> Omar Khayyam, *The Rubaiyat*

G is an almost sinister town. It seems to have soaked up some of the blood spilt in the course of millennia on the battlefields on both sides of the Hellespont, also known as the Dardanelles, a nexus of conflict since the demise of Troy.

In area it is not a small town. Parts of it are very old, with wooden villas weathered to silver-grey, graced in spring by lilac bushes, irises, flowering fruit trees and wisteria. They once belonged to Jewish townspeople. There are old Greek mansions too, and cottages with harled facades. The Greeks were forced to flee eight decades ago, in the aftermath of the Asia Minor Catastrophe. Their ancient, forgotten cities lie buried beneath new legends forged from the hellfire and hopelessness inscribed in the name 'Gallipoli'. On a rise overlooking the strait, a cemetery contains graves of French soldiers from the time of the Crimean War. Nearby, in midsummer, the mosque of Suleyman Pasha suffocates in the fragrance of its roses.

In contrast to the rambling impression of old neighbourhoods, the town's heart is small and pinched and lends itself to mean-ness. It is not possible to pass through the vortex of agencies selling coach tickets without being observed by the men sitting at tables outside tea houses and the more affluent citizens who preside over the bus companies and strategically placed hotels.

Such a town, provincial to the point of decadence, breeds its own varieties of tension, its own cravings. People don't escape from it. Traditions are entrenched in a kind of perverse loyalty that ends in stagnation. Self-destruction is a spectre haunting those obliged to stay.

 One form of escapism is gambling. Here the idle sons of wealthy fathers pass their nights at cards, their days in the dead sleep of compulsive losers. The nights sap their vitality and they become lethargic, animated only by the prospect of the game.

It was here, while completing a lengthy assignment as a journalist, that I recently had occasion to spend some time.

The eldest son of the town's wealthiest man (as I had been told) owned the hotel where I took a room. One of his brothers ran it for him. The owner was also an inveterate gambler, as I soon observed.

Sitting in the hotel lounge having my postprandial coffee, I would watch the young men who lodged upstairs come down one by one – three or four of them, wearing similar suits, almost interchangeable in looks and manner – and register with bleary eyes that it was day. My visit coincided with Ramadan, Islam's month of fasting, so the gamblers could neither eat nor smoke. Instead, they would ensconce themselves in armchairs with their prayer beads, and pass the afternoon in a state of suspended animation.

At three, or four, or five, their young patron would appear and park his silver-blue Mercedes outside the front windows. The gamblers would show flickerings of interest at this point: a glint in the eye, an acceleration in the click of prayer beads as the scion of the town's wealthiest man made his entrance.

His manner was imperious, but he had the same bleary eyes and blurring body as the others, the same pallid, puffy, unworked hands with a pinkie ring of cluster diamonds. His facial features were strongly delineated, particularly in profile. His appearance and bearing suggested qualities that might have been put to better use.

Curt greetings were exchanged, deferential on their part, perfunctory on his. He would sit for a time, restlessly running his black prayer beads through his fingers, visibly regaining vitality, while they all watched him for a sign. The moment he moved they were at his side, then they would depart together in the Mercedes, driving a few blocks this way and that to inspect the family's newest building sites and enterprises.

I noticed when they returned in the late afternoon that there was always a young woman sitting in the lounge, at the back towards the bar, with a discreet view of the street. She was a foreigner, whose appearance reminded me of Eastern European women I had met from time to time. There seemed to be a thread of unspoken communication between her and the young man, though usually he barely acknowledged her presence. The rest of his party were aware of her, however, and watched his reactions to her closely. If he acknowledged her, so did they.

According to the conventions of the fasting month, there was a further interval of waiting, until the mosque illuminations and the cannon signalled that it was time to dine. Then the patron would nod to the young woman, and she would go with the group to a nearby restaurant.

When they returned, all were in better spirits. The young woman would enter, smiling, at the young man's side. He ordered coffee for her, cigarettes, pistachios, and sometimes sat beside her for an hour watching television. The gamblers would group themselves about the pair, expectantly. If he talked to her a lot, they would react with bland smiles, but you could tell they were perturbed.

One night, they were perturbed to the point of vexation. He sat with her all evening and talked a lot. Sometimes the two of them laughed, and found pretexts to touch each other. His fingers brushed against her arm as he passed a dish of sweets. Her hair brushed his cheek as she explained something. His features had a gentler cast than I had seen before. Her obvious affection for him seemed less inexplicable.

But her victory that night, if that is the correct interpretation of what I saw, was a Pyrrhic one. At midnight a messenger arrived, the young man leapt to his feet, and the group of men moved as one, out the door and up and down the street, conferring urgently.

Sitting at the bar, I watched him hurry to his car and get in. He moved with unexpected grace and speed. Before his cohort could follow him, the young woman rushed out to the driver's door. He got out, surprised, and she flung her arms about his neck while the other men stood by impassively. He disengaged himself, got into the car and drove away. The others followed in another car.

That happened midway through my stay, and incidentally confirmed my suspicion that she occupied the room next door to mine. Usually she slipped in and out so quickly and quietly that I had never actually seen her come or go. On this occasion, obviously too distressed to be cautious, she grabbed her key from its hook behind the reception desk and ran upstairs. The key she took was hanging next to mine.

I tried to pinpoint when she had arrived. I'd first become aware of her, though not of how she looked, several nights before, when I'd spent the evening in my room. Through the wall, I'd heard two voices, male and female. I couldn't decipher the language or the words, only sounds and intonations. Her voice was more prevalent than his. The exchange that night went on for hours. She seemed to be asking many questions. Then the voices would lower into silence, and resume again, very low and monosyllabic. Everything I had witnessed since that night left me in no doubt as to who her visitor was.

I'd heard the shower running for a long time, then the clink of coffee cups outside their door. Shortly after that, someone knocked. There was an exchange of male voices through the door, then somebody left the room, presumably the young man who owned the hotel. I was sure by now that it had been him.

Intrigued as I had become by the curious enclave at the hotel, I'd begun to neglect my own assignment. It was difficult to ignore what was going on, or for that matter to ignore the girl. There was something about her. My journalistic instincts sniffed a story. My self-preservation instincts told me to back off, to watch and wait, but time was getting short. I was becoming frustrated at my own relative inactivity and, at the same time, impatient to know more about the events unfolding around me. By this time I had been at the hotel five days, and she, I estimated, for about the same.

The following night, an opportunity to approach her presented itself. I'd been unable to sleep, so I went downstairs at about three a.m. to take a stroll to the quay. Ferries ply all night across the strait. Their sirens punctuate that town's nocturnal soundscape. As I crossed the foyer, I saw her sitting there, dressed in baggy Turkish trousers and a flimsy blouse, half-illuminated by the night light. She was staring blankly at the clock behind the reception desk. The desk clerk was slumped forward, head on his arms, asleep.

'Hello,' I said, approaching her. 'Where are your friends?'

She started, and then answered me in English. I couldn't place her accent.

'They are at the casino.' She gestured upwards towards the window and across the street.

In a tall, new building behind the travel agencies, the top floor was illuminated, but the windows were masked by drapes. She looked at me dismissively and lit a cigarette.

When I returned from my walk, she'd gone upstairs. I drew aside the curtains in my room. Light from her windows outlined her shadow on the street. I glanced across at the casino windows. A man's silhouette was framed in one of them. I did not think it was the young woman's paramour. The man at the window looked shorter, and I thought I recognised him as one of the gamblers who lived in the hotel. As I watched, forgetting for the moment that I too could be seen, the whistles of the military patrol began to shrill, and then the drums that preceded the day's fasting rumbled in the street. The lights in the casino all went out abruptly. The curtains in the room next door snapped shut.

I wondered how long this situation could continue. Being at the periphery of their downward spiral was dissipating my energy. The young man was obviously the centre of a magnetic field. The gamblers were his creatures. But he needed them, too, he was addicted to the same pursuit. And what was the woman's part in it all? She looked intelligent and sensitive; she had a vivid face and eyes, the articulate movements of a dancer. Why was she wasting her time with him, in such a backwater?

I'd seen the sidearms they all carried and noticed the mixture of fear and contempt with which the brother who ran the hotel regarded them. I guessed that some of the money they gambled away so freely came from the labour of tenant farmers and people who were similarly exploited. Now the woman caught up in this circus seemed to be abdicating her identity, becoming one of the hangers-on whose purpose in life centred on this young man already going to seed. I could see her losing vitality, coming downstairs with dark smudges under her eyes. I couldn't tell how he really felt about her.

I could sense frustration growing in her. The following evening, finding her inexplicably alone at seven-thirty, I invited her, on a rash impulse, to have dinner with me. Without a word she stood up and accompanied me. I couldn't tell whether she was acting from inclination or a tactical gambit that had nothing to do with me. I was by now confused about my own motives in relation to her. Somehow commitments and loyalties formed elsewhere seemed to loosen and dissolve in the atmosphere of that town.

If I'd been hoping to find out who she was and where she came from, I was disappointed. She gave her name as 'Darya', which I thought was probably assumed.

'I'd rather not tell you' was all she would say of her country of origin. 'But English is not my first language, although I know it well.'

About the young man she was more forthcoming. Perhaps she needed to unburden herself.

'Have you known him long?' I asked abruptly. I noticed that she wasn't eating, although she smoked and drank water.

'Long enough.' (A pause.) 'Two years. But I see him seldom.'
'What is it that brings you back? You're not happy here.'
'You are no psychologist, but maybe I will tell you.'
She refilled her glass and took a sip of water.

'When I met him, it was different. You know, beginnings… It was as if we had known each other somewhere before, in some better place, when we were innocent. We gave each other something – maybe an image, an illusion, though it seemed more real than that, at the time… It made us so alive, to everything. Not like now. I think we were both desperate, before we met. You do impulsive things. Meeting him gave me back my energy, it made me want to live, to be constructive. I know what you see, and that is real, too, yet it's not all. There is another side to him – an artist, a lover, a sensibility – which is dying. I don't want to watch it happen, but I can't leave now. I can't let them win without a struggle.'

'You really think you'll win?'

'I can't afford to lose.'

'Why don't you leave, before he loses interest?'

'You're implying that I can't help him, that whether I stay or leave will make no difference to him. Perhaps it is too late to help myself, but I can't accept what I am seeing. If it is really true, then I will leave.'

'How long does it take to recognise the truth?'

She lit a cigarette and inhaled as if she hadn't heard me. My meal had gone cold before I noticed it in front of me, but my desire to learn more about her had dulled any appetite for food.

She stubbed out her cigarette before continuing. 'Always when I first arrive, I think it is all right. The first night, it is always new again. We are so happy. He talks about his projects, what he will make and build. He forgets them all, those men. We both forget. Then, when it is late, they come for him.'

'Why does he go with them?'

Instead of answering, she said, 'The second night is not so good. Then he starts to make excuses, shows me his despair. "I have a black job," he will say. "Not a normal life. But this I started many years ago. I must keep going. When I am forty, I will stop, get closer to the mosque."'

'Where will you be then?'

Again she looked evasive, then shrugged, feigning indifference.

In the street the next morning, I saw the young man walking with his father. The family resemblance was unmistakable. The father was leading his son by the hand, the old man's face a study in parental indulgence and pride, the son's gentle, reminding me not of the caged wolf I had sometimes glimpsed behind his languid facade in the hotel lounge – a feral, unpredictable quality Darya was aware of too – but of the docile pet lambs old men lead about in villages, completely trusting, doted on by their owners, unaware they are being fattened for the annual ritual slaughter that precedes the feast of Bayram, the culmination of the fasting month of Ramadan.

That night, I missed Darya in the hotel foyer. The old man was sitting there instead, complacently, a glint almost of triumph in his eye. The son appeared soon after, and remonstrated with him. The old man smiled a stubborn smile, but wouldn't budge.

I heard the voices for a short time in her room, late that night. I saw the watchers, waiting at the casino windows across the way.

By the next night she had gone. I asked the brother working on reception.

'Yes,' he said, 'she left today. Perhaps she knows it's too late, but I think she hasn't learned that yet. She will be back. She is one of them.'

'A gambler?' I asked, already knowing the answer.

'A gambler,' he said.

That night I lay awake, planning my departure, listening to her empty room, the drums.

Stopover in Budapest

The jagged sobs of a child in pain, sharpened by a note of fear, accompany a woman's shrieks, splintering the torpid summer noon. Far below the windows of the fifth-floor apartment, ragged poplars shed wisps of fibre resembling discoloured shreds of cotton dressing.

Inside, bloody footprints lead towards the bathroom. As the woman's high-pitched cries subside, the child's sobs become subdued. Madame Szusza emerges from the bathroom, dragging her ten-year-old daughter roughly by the arm. The girl's right foot is wadded in a bandage, and there is a strong smell of disinfectant.

'You see what she does?' Madame expostulates shrilly. 'She does this on purpose. To spite me.'

'What happened?' I murmur lamely.

'Glass! She stepped on broken glass!'

At the time of my sojourn, Hungary is still locked into the Draconian protocols of the Eastern bloc, and its citizens have little or no freedom of movement.

A few days earlier, Madame Szusza, whose spare room I am renting for a two-week stay in Budapest, had recounted excerpts from her life over a cup of expertly prepared espresso in her tiny living room, which was colourful and cosy with hand-woven rugs and folk art.

While working at the Italian embassy, she had fallen in love with a junior diplomat. Before she could tell him she was carrying his child, he had been abruptly transferred. Leaving her – she described an arc with her hand and forearm, suggesting the contour of a pregnant woman's abdomen, waxing like the moon – 'like this. With baby in the belly.'

The diplomat had phoned her now and then for several years, and even sent a little money. She had been unable to contact him by phone, or obtain a visa to travel abroad. She had smuggled messages and letters to him, until embassy staff who helped her do so were in due course replaced.

As time went by, hopes of a reunion with her daughter's father faded. Apart from the photographs she sent, he had never seen his child.

Madame Szusza's daughter is very beautiful – olive-skinned, long-limbed, with lustrous hair and hazel eyes. She is also rebellious to the point where it seems that she actively detests her mother. The tension between them is apparent in even the smallest daily transactions, such as the offering of food and drinks, which Maria makes a point of rejecting, forcing her mother to rant then plead before she'll accept any sustenance. This is all the more perverse in a growing child, who must surely have a hearty appetite.

It is a bitter irony that Madame Szusza should have given birth to a love child who seems to hate her.

Madame is quite unlike her daughter in appearance. She is petite and plump, with black-dyed hair piled in a beehive style. Her skirts are just a shade too short for modesty, her heels more than a shade too high for ease of gait or comfort.

She wears matching costume jewellery – necklace, earrings, bracelet – set with sparkling stones. 'A gift from my friend Omar, who comes here for his holidays.'

Madame now gives Maria's arm an emphatic little jolt, berating her in torrents of Hungarian. The girl looks sullen. Then her mother snatches up a small overnight bag and leads Maria out of the apartment.

Within the hour, Madame reappears, accompanied by a young man whom she introduces to me as Omar. Intent on departure, she bustles in and out of her room, dangly earrings flashing in the motes of slanting sunlight.

'I return in three days,' she tells me. Valise in hand, she moves towards the front door in a miasma of musky perfume, a trifle stale.

As she turns to exit, Omar closes the gap between them, an anticipatory palm placed firmly on her hip.

The Zeigarnik Effect

One section of the kitchen wall is a slightly denser shade of white than the rest. I am probably the only person aware of this. In fact, with the lapse of time, it is probably something discernible solely to the mind's eye rather than actually visible.

Much of what has happened in the interim has been elided from memory. For the decade that I lived abroad, I thought I had escaped, although it was not so much the house that I needed to flee. And yet, now that I'm back, I remember what interrupted the repainting of the kitchen wall more clearly than some of the events of the intervening years. It is only recently, having already experienced a personal version of this phenomenon, that I discovered it has a name: the Zeigarnik effect – a kind of memory bias whereby the details of an interrupted task or process are recalled more vividly than those of a completed one.

Unlikely as it may seem, what interrupted the repainting of the kitchen wall was a Hungarian film whose title eludes me. While I cannot account for the lasting impression it has left, I find that I can still project certain images – as fresh and clear-cut, as frozen in time as illustrations of ice crystals – onto the discoloured white wall. That I should feel impelled to do so at this juncture puzzles me, but the flashback may have been prompted by recent upheavals that have jolted me into redefining my attitude to walls, both actual and metaphorical.

Hungary – in particular, Budapest – holds a special fascination and significance for me, and that is presumably why I was so willing to drop the paintbrush and rush off to catch a film at an obscure, dingy suburban cinema that screened foreign-language features.

The film was about blind obsession, and love – a marriage be-tween an older woman and a younger man, a military officer, in Budapest before the Second World War. They appear to be deliriously in love, but her feeling is more intense than his – voluptuous, voracious, all-consuming. Her desire for him is insatiable. One of the scenes crystallised in memory takes place in a larder at a country retreat – a hunting lodge belonging to her family – where apples are being stored. In this setting, you can sense the chill of autumn in the air; you can smell the apples and taste the sharp sap of the juice as you bite into one, and they glow in the cold grey light as if burnished, their skins shading through gold to shiraz.

The woman is arranging apples on a table when her husband finds her there. Within moments of their encounter, their mutual intoxication sends the apples rolling across the floor along with the lovers. Such scenes have since become cinematic cliché – apples as symbols of abundance, or temptation, or whatever significance the context calls for or confers. But in the Hungarian film the scene is auric, ephemeral, evocative of Indian summer's acme and afternote.

So totally absorbed in each other is the pair that it seems their circle of joy is complete, but the woman – whom I shall call Marta – wants more. She wants the impossible – to give him a child, and in her desperate determination she conceives a plan. Another woman will bear Marta's husband's child, but it will then become Marta's. Although it cannot be Marta's biological child, the natural mother will relinquish it at birth by prior agreement.

Marta's family is wealthy. She is able to find a young woman of refinement (a music student – a violinist) who is poor enough and needy enough to agree to her plan. The young woman is tastefully outfitted by the older one in a wardrobe of gorgeous gowns in shades of copper, antique gold, rose, cinnamon, cerise, shiraz – and given her instructions.

The husband is embarrassed, reluctant to proceed with such a scheme. He tries to reassure Marta that they do not need a child to make their happiness complete, it is enough that they have each other, but Marta is by this time obsessed with her objective and will not be deterred.

Several social occasions ensue, in which the young woman, wearing her unaccustomed, exquisite, richly coloured gowns, spends time with Marta and her husband as a prelude to what Marta intends.

The private encounter between Marta's husband and the apprehensive, vulnerable young woman takes place at the hunting lodge. She has never been with a man before, and he is touched by her purity, modesty and beauty. The image of the young violinist tugs at his consciousness and begins to displace that of Marta, whose husband and the mother of his unborn child continue to meet in secret. The music student comes to exert a different kind of sway over him from that of his wealthy, older, domineering wife. The young woman's power over him is no less intense. It is the sovereignty of love that can offer only itself, without trappings. He feels a profound tenderness for her that he has never felt for his wife.

Marta, possessive, jealous and vigilant, cannot fail to become aware of these developments, but she clings to the belief that if she can contain herself until the birth of the child, the young woman can then be banished forever.

*

Tormented by her husband's defection, Marta writhes on a bed as if racked by birth pangs. The sounds of childbirth are heard from beyond the wall, where her husband, beside himself with concern and solicitude, is hovering as near as the midwife will permit to the young woman in labour.

Marta is waiting to pounce on the child, but her triumph is short-lived. Her husband is repelled by the way she has manipulated events, and his only care is for the well-being of the baby's natural mother.

Several years pass, and Hitler's armies invade Budapest. Consumed with venom as she once was with passion, Marta hatches another plan.

In the final scene, the young woman appears in a queue of deportees, all wearing yellow armbands with the Star of David, shuffling through bleak winter streets under guard, to be shipped off to death camps. The officer, still nominally Marta's husband, although he now leads a double life with the mother of his child, finds out too late to intervene.

This is what I see when I look at the dingy white wall, where the paint is slightly denser, and which, for some reason, after seeing the film, I did not finish repainting. Had I not interrupted my painting to see it, would I remember the film with such clarity? If I were to finish repainting the wall now, which would mean starting afresh, would I elide those cinematic images?

I have sometimes wondered what would happen if I were to see that film again. How much of what I recall is my own invention, my own film? But the opportunity for comparison has not so far arisen.

*

Yet why that film? Why then? Why now? 'Why then' at least has a credible answer. My son, born in the year I saw the film, was conceived in Budapest, under circumstances that now seem as remote, mysterious and unaccountable as the impression left by the film. The events of that time in Hungary may never be fully explained. It is similar to what happens when you try to recount the plot of a film. What is truly memorable, and why, mostly gets lost in translation. But I still remember the fat, fragrant roses, chubby as cherubs' feet and hands, smothering Gellert's Hill; the chalcedony hues of the Danube at dusk, and the peonies blooming – *punköszdi rosza* – in gardens cradling drab wooden villas in quiet back streets of old neighbourhoods.

What is it that prompts me to lay out images like cards: vivid fragments of a film; fleeting impressions of a city; the enigmatic strangeness of events I still cannot decipher – cards from a broken deck? Is it because my own *ménage à trois* recently came to an end – although it was not a triangle in any conventional sense? There was an older woman and a younger man, it is true, but she never aspired to have a child with him, nor he with her. And theirs was a brief love affair, destined to evolve into a passionate friendship, not without its perils, but chaste. It's another story, quite unlike the film scenario, except in the impotent envy the older woman once felt for the younger one who supplanted her in her lover's affections. Yet it is futile to envy after all, and the younger woman is so angular and unalluring, so frozen into conventional poses, that it is tempting to see their liaison more as a *mariage de convenance* than one inspired by passion or affinity.

Perhaps it's simply the consciousness of mutability – what this does to passions and affinities – that brings the film to mind. And because, although it's summer, the day is tinged with a foretaste of autumn, overcast, its muted luminosity imbued with the sense of something golden drawing to a close, the glow of Indian summer fading to long, dark winter nights. Perhaps love affairs that have died an untimely death are also subject to the Zeigarnik effect in the way they linger in the psyche as persistent, clamorous regret. For is it not remarkable that every detail of such a doomed yet fervently desired liaison seems to assume a clarity and lustre out of all proportion to its evanescence?

It may be, too, that the filmic images wordlessly affirm for me an essential truth that seems to underlie what has happened – that love cannot be reconciled with or to or by walls. It can neither be confined nor kept at bay by them, neither locked in nor locked out. And so devotion between friends somehow surmounts obstacles, and lovers find that walls dissolve between them, fluid as images on film, captured in flight and stored as stills to be apprised: haunting, untranslatable.

Having transferred its palimpsest of secrets to this other site, what remains to deter me from repainting the wall? Before deciding what to do, I should like to know: does the wall represent the future or the past? Or is it – a sobering thought – a metaphor for the continuous present? Has it become internalised, a state of being immured in one's own limitations, as Marta was in the film?

*

The unresolved implications continue to perplex me, and the hidden heart of the matter, impassive as this shabby, once-white kitchen wall, continues to elude me, until there comes a time when, distracted by other concerns, I walk past the wall without registering its presence. Until one sparkling morning when, charmed by the birdsong streaming with sun rays through the open kitchen door, I am standing in rapt contemplation of the gold and green tangle of chlorophyll beyond. As I stand in the shaft of song and light, something appears in my peripheral vision. At first I mistake it for the flicker of leaves or wings – but no. There is what looks like shadow writing on the wall. I turn to read the inscription:

GET A LIFE!

Before my eyes, the ephemeral words dissolve in the shimmering fusion of sunlight and birdsong.

No Such Address

Do people grow to resemble their houses, or is it the other way round?

In the case of Misha's and Alexei's family home, there could be no neat correlation between house and occupants, as the brothers could not have been more dissimilar. Misha, gregarious by nature, was a prankster whose party tricks amused and sometimes scandalised staid gatherings of conservative Russian émigré youth. His elder brother Alexei, taciturn, saturnine, preferred to spend his leisure in solitude by the mud-coloured river, catching catfish which he fed to his tom cat, Bars. It was no party trick, but he had been known to fly into a state of wordless fury or blind frustration, stabbing his catch with a filleting knife, slashing it to slivers.

If the house resembled either of its occupants, it had to be Alexei. Situated behind a disused cemetery, encroached upon by sombre Chinese elms, it was a place of green gloom. The high windows admitted murky light, absorbed by the walls, which were also greenish and other nondescript shades where the paint had darkened over time with oxidation and grime.

Kitty wondered what the house had been like when Misha's family had filled it – his parents, grandparents and seven siblings. Surely it had overflowed with vitality then: sounds of food preparation and chatter, scolding and laughter. The rooms would have been lighter when the paint was fresh, and the curtains laundered regularly, although the crushed-velvet drapes that flanked the rotting cream lace were also a bilious shade of slime green. She imagined white table linen, vivid accents and splashes of colour: cushions, upholstery, Oriental rugs, flowers… Now the two brothers, adult orphans, camped in the spaces vacated by parents and siblings. Their presence wasn't ample enough to compensate for the absences.

Kitty had been invited to dinner because she was Delia's sister. Delia was friends with Misha's fiancée, Tamara; so Delia and her fiancé, Nigel, were the intended guests. Kitty had been an afterthought on Tamara's part. With one eye on Alexei, she now suspected. It was only a matter of months since Kitty had moved to the city from the country town where she and Delia had grown up.

Approaching the house via the old cemetery road for the first time on an autumn evening, with the leaves on the Chinese elms a jaundiced yellow matching the fading sky, was a slightly unnerving experience. The candle light inside dulled the greenish tinge without dispelling the gloom. Kitty felt claustrophobic on entering, despite the spacious, high-ceilinged, sparsely furnished rooms, but even if she'd been handed the car keys she couldn't have fled, because from the moment she set eyes on Misha, she seemed to have fallen under his spell. She was at a loss to account for the unprecedented effect he had on her, and simultaneously dismayed that she couldn't muster the least resistance to the peculiar sensation his presence induced in her.

It was hardly Misha's fault. He had only made eye contact for a moment when he greeted her, but that had been enough to demolish her sense of reality. She moved through the evening as if suspended on invisible strings.

Alexei seemed sociable enough at first, helping mercurial Misha and bubbly Tamara prepare a sort of Russian stir-fry with noodles to accompany the dumplings and stuffed cabbage rolls Tamara had made that morning. But once they were all seated at table, the shadows cast by the candles flickering eerily on the walls, he seemed to retreat into himself. Kitty's attempts to engage him were futile, although she did manage to ascertain that he had a normal, regular job – well, if you could call importing caviar normal. She'd tasted some for the first time before the meal, with a vodka aperitif. 'Russian Vegemite,' Misha had quipped, catching her eye. Kitty had almost choked at that point, and had to be thumped on the back, mortified.

Alexei, while unwilling to chat, was not oblivious to the non-verbal cues passing between Kitty and Misha. As he watched, from under his brows, his brother's covert appraisal of Kitty, and her blushing attempts to evade eye contact, a sardonic mask slipped over his features. It fitted him well, for Misha always got the girls, but why should Alexei care? Women made him uncomfortable. Still, did he wonder how it would feel to be the one sought after, for once?

Delia and Nigel – an aspiring academic who tended to take himself rather too seriously – were touching each other's thighs under the table. Tamara was her usual witty, effervescent self, holding the gathering together with her chatter and anecdotes, her delicate teardrop earrings flashing beside her pert-featured face and tilted green eyes. Her ancestry was not Russian, but Tartar. If she noticed Misha's gaze straying across the pickled mushrooms and cucumbers, the herrings in brine, to linger on Kitty's startled features, she gave no sign.

After the *zakuski* and main course, Alexei, Tamara and Misha excused themselves and retired to the kitchen to prepare the sweets. Before exiting, Tamara had dropped an old LP on the ancient gramophone to entertain them while they waited. It was a recording of a torch singer of the Soviet era. Delia, who had studied Russian at university, translated one of the lyrics for Nigel and Kitty:

> Coachman, don't urge the horses on:
> I've nowhere else to hurry to,
> there's no one else for me to love,
> so don't whip up the horses…

The melancholy old romance seemed to echo the ambience of the house in its evocation of a bleak night and deserted streets pervaded by a sense of stagnation and despondency. Where were the balalaikas, the hectic gaiety Kitty had been half expecting?

Tamara soon returned with Alexei, bearing plates of flaming Crêpes Suzette which they placed in front of the guests with a flourish, in a parody of sideshow magicians.

'Where's Misha?' asked Delia.

'He'll be here in a moment,' said Tamara, changing the record on the turntable. 'I give you – Vertinsky!' she announced airily.

As a nineteen-thirties cabaret number struck up, into the room burst Misha, frocked and bejewelled, his amber-brown eyes elegantly though heavily dramatised with eyeliner and eyeshadow, his *faux* lashes mascaraed, lips a sultry moue of peony, framed by a long, dark, silky wig with a fringe brushing his high-arced brows. His lithe build and olive complexion were complemented by a slinky black sheath, though the jutting bosom would have to be fake.

Glitzy bracelets and rings caught the light as he minced around the faded Oriental rug in time to the music, wearing a pair of Tamara's stilettos. At every pause in the lyrics, he struck an attitude, glancing archly over his shoulder at Kitty.

Kitty was devastated afresh. Aghast yet mesmerised. Tamara looked amused, but she had seen it all before. These antics were already beginning to pall. As one in a trance, Kitty gazed at the silhouette on the wall as Misha thrust out a hip or rotated a naked shoulder. He had never so much as laid a finger on her, other than to clasp her hand briefly in greeting, yet Kitty felt ravished by his presence, by the current of intense energy he was directing at her.

Approaching the table, Misha eased on a pair of elbow-length black gloves, kissed his fingertips to his audience, slid an index finger under Kitty's chin to tilt her face upward, let his painted lips hover over hers for an instant, gave a brief laugh, then made his exit.

Nigel assumed a patronising expression, as if bored by such cheap theatrics. Kitty flushed with embarrassment that Delia had noticed her gauche reaction, as had Alexei.

'Are you okay?' Delia asked.

Kitty nodded uncertainly.

'You mustn't take any notice of Misha,' Tamara said kindly. 'It's just his way of releasing tension. Just a bit of fun.'

But Kitty felt as if a demon had wormed its way into her consciousness since she'd arrived at this house. A demon whose human form was slim, boyish, smooth-skinned and tawny-eyed, taunting her with the mysterious energy she found so compelling.

During the drive home, Kitty shrank into the back seat as Delia's and Nigel's thigh-fondling became more urgent in front, despite the restraining seat belts.

When a few days had elapsed, Kitty called Delia and asked, in what she hoped was a casual tone, for Misha's and Alexei's address. 'I'd like to say thanks for the dinner,' she said. 'You know, send an old-fashioned card or a note…'

Delia, after a hesitant pause, dictated the details.

A week later, Kitty's note was returned with the words scrawled across it 'No such address'.

Horns of a Dilemma

Leningrad, pre-glasnost. The streets are treacherous with melting snow and thawing ice. The season is bleak, the city chill, remote as a nineteenth-century aquatint of itself. The wintry afternoon light is strained dully through voluminous layers of cloud.

I've been stalking my quarry for three days now, and it seems I have run her to earth. You can see her clearly through the window of this café, leaning against the stone wall outside the bookshop across the street.

It's time to cross the road and take a closer look…

It is as I suspected.

Tears are pouring down her cheeks and soaking into her pale woollen scarf. She doesn't appear to belong in this place.

Inside the shop, a man with a ferocious black beard is fossicking among old books, lost in contemplation of the titles in Cyrillic.

The two may not have anything to do with each other, but one nevertheless senses that there is some connection. They may or may not be foreigners, it's difficult to tell.

Her watery blue-green eyes and general appearance make it hard to say whether she's a local. Similarly, plenty of Russians look like him. Perhaps their clothes are an indication. Although there is nothing startling about them, they don't appear to be of Soviet manufacture.

Anyway, she is weeping.

Why is she weeping? At least one person wants to know, apart from me.

A faded, shabbily dressed, weatherbeaten woman of indeterminate age detaches herself from the purposefully moving stream of pedestrians to approach the young woman. 'What's the matter?' she asks abruptly.

The young woman understands, and answers hesitantly.

(So she could be a local after all. Does it matter? Do we need to know? But I think she's a foreigner.)

'N-nothing,' she sniffles.

The passer-by is not so easily put off. 'There must be something,' she insists.

The young woman becomes embarrassed, agitated.

The other woman doesn't budge. Clearly she is not going to depart until her curiosity has been satisfied. Meanwhile, I've edged as close as I can. The two women are not aware of my presence.

The young woman begins, through a fresh spasm of sobs and sniffles. 'Well, it's… my husband…'

'Got another woman, has he?' asks the older one, a knowing glint in her eye.

'N-not exactly, no…'

'Then what…?'

'Well, you see…h-he doesn't love me,' she stammers, mortified.

'Is that all?'

'H-he never did.' A muffled sob escapes. 'He was in love with someone here, when he was a student. I think… he still is…'

'Well,' replies the other matter-of-factly. 'Put horns on him then. Simple as that! Why not just put horns on him? You'll feel much better then.'

The young woman is perplexed. What on earth is this person suggesting? Her face crimsons with comprehension. Confusion registers in her expression. How could she think of such a thing? Besides, it's not as if he's…*done* anything. Not as far as she knows, that is. Anyway, that's not the point. She wants him to love *her*. That wouldn't change the way he feels about her, doing what this woman says…

(This is what I think she thinks. You see, it is a compulsion of mine to decipher the workings of people's minds.)

'Ah,' the other woman is saying, 'life's like that. During the war, there were real stories I could tell you. Why, even me. My daughter.

Never saw the father again. He went away, never came back. Killed at the front, most likely… But I don't cry about it. I have my daughter, we have our lives to live. Why waste tears?' She glances sharply at the stranger. 'You feel better now, don't you? Just do as I say,' she advises firmly. 'Put horns on him.'

She squeezes the young woman's hand and merges with the briskly moving current of passers-by.

The young woman with watery eyes looks around, suddenly lost. Where did the brusque, kindly woman go? Had she imagined her entirely? Instead, she sees that on the frozen pavement near her feet a man lies on his back, insensate. A half-smoked cigarette, the tip still glowing, hangs from slack lips. His face is unshaven. His arms are loosely crooked across his chest, his knees bent upwards in an inverted V. She didn't see him fall. She's heard about such people, taking a short cut to oblivion via the vodka bottle. She even imagines she can understand why.

It's like a dream. She isn't sure what's real any more. She can do nothing for the man. He is at a stage past caring.

So preoccupied is she with the inert figure at her feet that she still doesn't notice me. I've moved close enough to touch her, if I wanted to. But I don't need to touch her yet. My efforts are concentrated instead on making her the gift of an idea. What is the idea, you ask? Perhaps you will understand if I show you what she does with it.

The young woman glances over her shoulder through the frosty bookshop window at the bearded man.

(So it seems they are connected.)

Her imagination does a small involuntary skip, and for a fleeting instant horns appear and disappear on his head. What kind were they, quick! She only caught a glimpse of them. Too late! But what kind of horns would suit him best? Bull horns, in the style of the Spanish arena? No, too Mediterranean. Goat horns? Tempting, yes, but no. Buffalo? No, wrong type. Something dense and foresty. Stag? Getting closer. That's it! Moose horns!

She fixes a pair of moose horns on his head and begins to giggle.

Soon she is laughing helplessly until the tears begin to flow again. Nobody stops to ask her why she is laughing.

The bearded man emerges from the shop with a bundle of roughly wrapped books under his arm. 'What's so funny?' he asks gruffly.

(He is speaking a language I understand imperfectly, but I get the picture well enough. Here, I shall improvise.)

'Well?'

'Oh, nothing,' she chortles. 'That woman, you, life!' She laughs again.

He doesn't understand. She can see him puffing up with indignation.

'Well, I'm glad you find me such a joke,' he begins peevishly.

'Oh,' she says, 'you wouldn't understand, but the thought of you with horns…!'

His face flushes deeply. His features are heavy with self-righteous rage. In that instant, she wonders if she ever loved him at all. She wonders why it seemed so important for him to love her.

She begins almost to dance along the street, perilously close to losing her footing on the thin ice. She imagines horns sprouting at random from the heads of passing men and giggles to herself at her own invention. 'It's easy to put horns on them,' she thinks. 'I could do it to all of them if I wanted to.'

Behind her in the distance, her husband's voice (this must be the husband) reaches her as a bellow. 'Have you taken leave of your senses?' he rumbles.

'You can't catch me,' she shrieks. 'I'm fast, I'm free! You'll never catch me now!'

She imagines she hears the thud of feet (or is it hooves?) pursuing her, and lets out a shrill cry of anticipation. Maybe at last, just once, he will acknowledge that she matters more to him than books and scholarship and the academy. In her mind she is not, at that moment, the unhappy and neglected student-wife of an aspiring professor, but a reckless and unlikely Daphne being pursued improbably over ice by an incongruously horned Apollo.

Such is the capacity of unconscious desires to assert themselves irrespective of circumstance. And you no doubt wonder how I know her so intimately. Let me tell you only this. She is closer to me than she will ever be to him.

Had she looked back in time, she would have seen a bearded, hornless Dostoevskian figure turn a corner, a bundle tucked beneath his arm, and become lost to view.

As you see, the whole idea got out of hand, and so did she. I had to let her go, although she hasn't seen the last of me.

It isn't easy, being a writer in Russia.

The Tale of the Girl and the Tiger

Once upon a time in Siberia, when animals and humans could understand each other's languages, there lived a girl and a tiger. Hunters had killed the tiger's mother when he was only a few weeks old, and then given the orphaned cub to the girl. When this happened, Altis herself was still a child, barely ten years of age, living in the forest with her father, a craftsman whose livelihood was carving furniture and animals from wood.

Altis, whose name means 'golden', was allowed to raise the cub as she saw fit. He soon outgrew the milk she fed him from her father's cow, and would have eaten the cow instead, had the hunters not kept him supplied with fresh meat. He was a resplendent, ferocious-looking tiger, but Altis trained him so well not to harm humans or their domestic animals that he curbed his natural instincts for her sake.

As he grew larger and more independent, he learned to hunt for himself. He would go off in search of prey, and return when his appetite was sated, sinking to his haunches and stretching out with a deep, satisfied purring sound in front of the woodsman's fireplace.

He would watch over Altis as she slept – a most unusual thing for a tiger to do. This was in fact no ordinary tiger, for in a past life he had been a young hunter, the most renowned in the *taigá*, but he had abducted a shaman's daughter and, as punishment, the shaman had stolen the young man's spirit and given it to an unborn tiger cub. So his spirit was that of a fearless young hunter whose audacity had cost him his life.

Altis knew nothing of this. She knew only that the tiger was her dearest friend, who accompanied her whenever she went into the forest and protected her from danger. The hunters recognised her tiger, and took care not to harm him.

When Altis turned sixteen, her father went to see the matchmaker who lived at the edge of the forest, to ask her to find his daughter a suitable husband. But when the prospective bridegroom, bearing gifts, was brought to their cottage, the tiger growled a warning at him and prepared to spring at the young man's throat. As the suitor reached for his weapon, Altis leapt in front of the tiger, spreading her arms to protect her beloved companion.

The suitor fled, humiliated and enraged, vowing vengeance on the tiger. Altis stroked her pet's head, and two tears fell on his soft, deep fur.

'Don't be sad,' growled the tiger. 'I'll never leave you.'

Altis knew her father would not rest until she was safely married, but she feared for her tiger at the hands of a jealous bridegroom. She knew she should also be worried about the bridegroom, as the tiger was equally prone to jealousy. She did not know what to do.

One morning soon after this, the tiger accompanied her into the forest as if to guard her while she gathered berries, but then led her on a long journey to where the shaman lived. They reached the shaman's tent only at nightfall. He emerged, clad in animal skins and looking more like a beast than a man.

The tiger behaved very strangely, crouching in front of the shaman and creeping towards him on his belly, hanging his head as if begging forgiveness.

The shaman folded his arms and looked down sternly at the unhappy tiger, then strode off into the darkness for a time. When he returned, he gazed deep into the eyes of first the tiger, then the girl. For a long while he was silent, as if pondering something, then he bent to whisper in the tiger's ear. The tiger glanced up at Altis in sorrow and wonder.

With a sign, the shaman took Altis aside and sat with her for a long time without breaking his silence. When he finally spoke, she listened closely to his words, then she, too, lapsed into a profound silence. At length she sighed, like someone who has just come to a difficult decision, or someone just awakening from sound, refreshing slumber. She looked up at the shaman and nodded slightly, as if in assent.

Gesturing to them to follow him, the shaman showed the girl and the tiger to a special tent whose interior was lined with rugs, their colours quickening in the flickering light of oil lamps. Then the shaman withdrew, murmuring to himself in a manner halfway between speech and song.

Altis took off her kerchief and unbound her long, thick, golden braids. Her hair hung like a silken shawl, burnished by the lamplight to rich russet, barred with darker shadows.

They could hear the whisper of the shaman's moccasins as he wove in circles around the outside of the tent, his voice intoning incantations in a language Altis could not recognise, to the sporadic accompaniment of little bells he wore on his wrists and ankles. But as their trance deepened, the tiger and the girl heard only each other's breathing, like the sighing exhalations of a young birch forest in spring, and saw only each other's eyes, catching the light like forest pools where moonbeams filter down through the canopy.

Altis could feel her arms becoming stronger, her torso melting as if taking on a different form, long and lithe and silky, with velvet striations of shadow, and then she seemed to sink into a deep, mysterious dream state, in which she imagined she was coursing through the wooded valleys with her tiger, weightless with joy.

As morning light stole gently through the leaves, the shaman watched with narrowed eyes as two sleek shadows left the tent where his guests had spent the night – two tiger forms that moved with grace and strength, until, striped in the rays of the rising sun, breaking into a joyous, loping stride, shoulder to shoulder they vanished into the forest whence they had come.

Reading Rilke

She glances at him as he explains the reason for his request, but her mind keeps shying off at a tangent. He seems to have no inkling of the images taking up defensive positions behind her eyes.

'My daughter now lives with her mother in Germany. They have migrated too. But in any case I have always admired the classics of German literature and music. The German philosophers, also, are very dear to me…'

An eight-year-old girl in a different, distant Germany is afraid of what hunger is doing to her. She wishes she could forget what she's been taught. That it's wrong to show weakness. Wrong to steal. German children do not show weakness, because they belong to a superior race.

If she were not a German child, it would not be wrong to go out to the countryside, to enter other people's fields, where there might be some nuts lying under the walnut trees, something to stop the gnawing hunger. She wouldn't let pride stop her from knocking on a farmhouse door to beg a glass of milk, a crust of bread. If she were an English child, for instance. English children, French children, Russian children could do that sort of thing. This helps to explain why the English, the French, the Russians, are losing the war, as the school director reminds her and her classmates daily.

'…just make coffee first,' she hears herself saying, moving blindly towards her small galley for refuge. But there is no wall she can hide behind, just a row of cupboards topped by a bench. She is as exposed as an eight-year-old girl on the streets of Berlin in 1945.

'It's the pronunciation. I have problems with the pronunciation,' he is saying. 'When I try to learn a new language, I want most of all to hear the poetry composed in that language. That is why I ask you to read Rilke for me. If you don't mind.'

Why should she mind? Why should it be so difficult to read her own language? The war had ended more than sixty years ago. But how had it ended for her, and when? She has heard it said by people who weren't there that not all the Russian soldiers who 'liberated' Berlin were barbarians. Everybody who had been there then knew otherwise, and in case they were in any doubt, the radio kept reminding them. How could one forget such things? Besides, she had seen them with her own eyes, the armies of the East, looking and sounding like wild beasts – hungry, haggard, angry, unshaven, and terrifying in their foreignness. They were nothing like the German soldiers she had seen parading, with their immaculate uniforms and sense of discipline. That was how civilised people looked!... She has read that the German invaders of Russia behaved worse than beasts, but one of her uncles was with them, and he was no beast...

'So I have chosen three poems from Rilke. If you will let me record you reading them, I can listen and learn from your pronunciation.'

Two hands are not enough to protect you from seeing and hearing. You have to choose whether to cover your eyes or your ears.

'Which poems have you chosen?' The answer is immaterial, but she must play for time to compose herself.

If she closes her eyes tightly, she can put her hands over her ears, but two small hands cannot shut out the rumble and vibration of tanks, the sound of boots on the cobblestones, the screams of fleeing women and children. (German women and children, who must at all times show their strength. But who now instead show terror, anguish.) She hears the brutes speaking. The voices of beasts of prey. They are as desperately hungry as the women and children. And they are winning the war.

'We shall drink the coffee, then I will read.'

How long had it been before the rich smell of coffee returned? Probably, the Americans had brought it. Her parents would drink it as if receiving a sacrament, inhaling the aroma with half-closed eyes, briefly transported to a time when there had been no need for the unnatural silence between them.

'Have you ever been to Germany?'

'No, but I hope I will go one day. To see my daughter, if she remembers me.'

'But why learn German? What is your purpose?'

'In Russia, we believe that culture is carried in language, and that to be educated, you must know other languages and literatures, especially those of Europe: France, Germany, England, Italy... I study these to educate myself, and for the pleasure, yes, the profound pleasure it brings me.'

She knows with certainty that nothing could have induced her to learn Russian. She had simply been caught off guard when asked to do this favour for a friend of a friend. But even now, she would be hard put to find a convincing excuse to refuse.

'So – we should begin.'

They move a little closer under the circle of light cast by the standard lamp, the grey head and the dark-haired, younger one.

'Ah! "*Der Panther*"'. Everybody knows "*Der Panther*".' It is a poem about a caged panther, pacing to and fro behind the bars which impinge on his vision, at the same time as they limit his freedom of movement, his entire life.

Strange, therefore, he thinks, since the poem is so well known, that she should stumble slightly on the second-last line. He should have given her more time to ready herself, but he had assumed she'd need no preparation.

Strange, she thinks, that her eyes should blur the familiar words. For a fleeting moment she felt she had changed places with the panther.

> Wearied by interminable bars,
> his vision comprehends nothing beyond.

But she has a check-up with the optometrist every year. Long ago, in Germany, she was told that her poor eyesight was due to wartime food shortages. Critical vitamin deficiencies, they said, in the developmental phase.

Reading the next poem, '*Die Erblindende*' – 'Going Blind' – about a woman losing her vision, her throat seems to open to allow her voice to pass unimpeded. The light glints fleetingly on the thick, owlish lenses she wears, as her involuntary glance flickers over him. His face is suffused with pleasure at having so dear a wish granted. To find a reader for Rilke's words in a country where he knows almost nobody...

His evident pleasure seems to ignite a corresponding spark in her as she reads the lines:

> upon her eyes, made luminous by joy,
> light moved as on the surface of a pool.

His final request is for '*Archaïsche Torso Apollos*'. 'An Archaic Torso of Apollo'. Predictably, she thinks. But reads with unexpect-ed warmth. After the last line has entered the tiny microphone, she sits with the open book on her lap, still resonating with the words. Exactly like an instrument as the last note fades into silence, he thinks.

The ending of this poem has become a commonplace: 'You must change your life. (*Du musst dein Leben ändern.*)' And yet these words had the power to move her when she uttered them just now. Strange.

The moment passes, and she closes the book, but her face is open, reflective, luminous.

He stands to leave.

She looks him in the eye for the first time. 'I never realised what a pleasure it can be to read the poems aloud. From now on, I will always do so. Thank you for making me see this.'

Her initial reluctance to read Rilke aloud to him still puzzles him, but he sees that she is indeed moved. No doubt the poems hold pleasant memories for her, he thinks. He steps lightly into the night, the recording – a wish granted, a gift – nestled in his breast pocket.

II

Curlew Country

Although Bush Stone-curlews can fly, they are ground dwellers, whose choice of sustenance and camouflage of cryptic plumage equip them for this habitat.

Voices in the Wind

At nine o'clock on the Friday night the island's generator failed. The men had gone to the mainland for their night off. The sea was turbulent. The manager was away, which left only Mara at the helm, ostensibly to cook for a bunch of laid-back writers on retreat, but also to take charge in the event of an emergency.

Bleary-eyed guests were still at the dining tables, plying themselves and each other with beer, wine and spirits as belated recompense for the heaving seas of the morning crossing. Some members of the company were giving voice to the fears induced by finding themselves in a boat that had seemed no match for vertiginous crests and troughs, when the lights lurched into a series of spasms: on/off/on/off. As inexplicably as it had faltered, the power was restored. Most of the guests were too disoriented to register Mara's exit into the night, clutching the keys to the admin hut. Her usually serene face was set and pale, but the back-up system had kicked in, the lights were on for the time being, the co-ordinator of the weekend retreat and a couple of volunteers were dishing up the sticky date pudding, and a convivial atmosphere permeated the cosy hub of the island's only accommodation.

Outside the comfort zone, clouds scudded across the face of a late-rising moon, the sea gnawed uneasily at the intertidal rocks, palm fronds rasped against each other in a discourse of harsh fricatives, leaves of eucalypts were restive, stirred to sibilant exchanges. Beneath the tension of this surface activity lay an unnerving sense of expectancy.

A couple of hours later, one of the men who'd gone to the mainland on leave appeared out of the wild night, summoned by Mara, his face raw from the windy crossing, and went straight to the shed housing the generator.

The guests dispersed to their bungalows, where the hardier souls sat out on the verandas, drinking, musing, chatting before turning in. Our cabin was the only one left from an earlier generation – fibro on a concrete slab with a rainwater tank at one end almost the height of the low roof. We were sheltered from the wind by the row of bungalows on the foreshore, by dunes away to one side and a fringe of casuarinas between us and the sea. The conversation was flowing in spurts and gushes, becoming desultory before flaring up again.

I was reflecting on an incident that had occurred late that afternoon, as the sun was slipping behind mounds of dark cloud along the horizon. I'd set out towards the spit at one end of the nearby beach, where the rocks shelved in layers, bridging the intertidal zone, and the land behind rose to a bluff, covered in speargrass, topped by pandanus.

At a certain point on the way to the spit, I'd been stopped in my tracks by what felt like an invisible wall – a field of force, an alignment of energies. At the point where this happened, a white heron or egret was fossicking in the small rock pools, apparently oblivious of the charged atmosphere.

Among the pandanus on the bluff above, something was stirring. The rustlings were not caused by the breeze, and sounded faintly sinister and hostile. I heard a few rusty carks from crows, caught sight of what looked like a Brahminy kite, yet could not shrug off the sensation that I was being observed. But by whom? Or what?

While aware that this island had a history of brutal dispossession involving the forcible removal of its Indigenous custodians, I knew no details of those events. However, the invisible resistance I had encountered before reaching the spit prompted the thought that my presence there might be a transgression. I didn't know what had happened in that place, and I knew nothing about the people who had belonged there. Troubled by a sense of foreboding, I turned back. As I retraced my steps, the atmosphere of latent yet nameless phobia dissipated.

*

It was around midnight outside our cabin, and only one other woman and I were left sitting under the awning. The activity at the other bungalows had all but ceased. We could hear possums scurrying about on the ground among the coconut palms. Then soundlessly a curlew emerged into the penumbra cast by our single light. Moving towards my chair, it fixed uncanny shaman eyes on me like wild half-moons, pupils dilated.

I knew what curlews were said to portend. Some Indigenous people believe curlews to be messengers from the other world – spirit birds, psychopomps, couriers of souls. While feeling privileged that this bird had no fear of me, I wondered why it had singled me out.

Approaching so close that I could have touched it, the curlew took a few more steps on its spindly legs until it was in the shadow of the table beside me, still watching me intently. Curlews are creatures of darkness and obscurity, of liminal zones, not only spiritually but physically. Their tapered bodies and tawny streaked and speckled plumage can camouflage them to resemble sand dunes, tree bark, dead branches and grasses. By day they escape detection by freezing in postures that make them indistinguishable from their surroundings.

After a few minutes, the mysterious visitor withdrew, leaving me wondering what its presence might have signified.

Although I resisted the temptation to regard the bird as some kind of portent, as I lay in a hypnagogic state between sleeping and waking, sensing the play of intertidal energies in my own consciousness, I seemed to hear voices in the wind. The voices had a disembodied quality as if coming from the ether, and were intermittently drowned out by the sounds of the sea and air currents passing through foliage. They possessed the timbre and tone and pitch of women's and children's voices, coming from some liminal time and place. Their cadences were those of people grieving.

In the morning, I casually asked my two cabin mates if they'd heard voices during the night, but they shook their heads.

When I walked along the beach late on the second afternoon, the sky had been clarified by wind and rain to a wintry purity. The mainland coast and the hills and mountains lunging away into the hinterland were vividly defined in violet, indigo and cobalt, while the horizon's western rim simmered with liquid gold.

Again I approached the point where I had been repulsed the previous day. The white bird flew up, startled, but I sensed no resistance to my passage on this occasion. Nevertheless, I turned back. Dusk was falling, and there was a brooding undercurrent in the air, too diffuse to be called a sense of foreboding, but clearly not welcoming.

That evening around the dining tables as the wine flowed freely, I heard a loud-voiced woman asking another member of the company if he'd found the cave that lay somewhere just beyond the spit I had failed to reach.

She had recently attended an open day on the island, where visitors had been told that the cave was used as a site of grisly punishment by one of the first foreigners to annex the place for raising livestock. Any signs of non-compliance the Indigenous residents displayed towards the terms of dispossession imposed by the pastoralist were met with the utmost brutality. Indigenous men, whose ancestral home the island had been for millennia, were chained by their necks to the cave walls, and left there as the tide flooded in.

After dinner, when the chatter from other cabins had died down, the curlew came again to where I was sitting outside, and lingered, observing me as before. The wind had abated, though not entirely. Later, lying wakeful in the ionised atmosphere, I listened again for the voices I fancied I'd heard the previous night, but the only sound disturbing the fretting tide was the chorus of curlews. Not the drawn-out wail from the spirit realm that is said to portend a death, but the agitated flurry of voices one hears when they all cry at once, as if in alarm and warning.

Love Me Tender

Rhonda and Dolly were their names, and they were best friends. Rhonda lived with her dad, and Dolly lived with her mum. Although they were only twelve – or rather, because they were only twelve – the girls were already the talk of the town.

They had been seen riding in cars with boys, and when Clive Jarrett, an apprentice mechanic at O'Leary's garage, got his first car with the help of a loan from his dad, it was no time at all before Rhonda and Dolly were making tongues wag as they cruised the streets after school in the back seat of Clive's two-tone '64 Ford Falcon sedan. On these daylight jaunts, Clive's mate, Bruce Blake, a builder's labourer, would sit in front.

On Saturday nights, the girls again made a foursome with Clive and Bruce. Shopkeepers shook their heads as the dream machine roared the length of the small town's main street at full throttle, did a wheelie outside the railway station and repeated the performance in reverse on the other side of the median strip. Rhonda hung out of the front passenger window, hair streaming, while Dolly, in the back seat with Bruce, laughed and waved to people she knew. What did eighteen-year-old boys with money in their pockets and a hot car to ride in want with two girls still in primary school? It could only be One Thing.

Rhonda, the dominant one of the pair, was unabashed by reproving looks, and Dolly took her cue from her friend. They didn't give a hoot what people said or thought. So many boys found them irresistible, they felt they'd gone way beyond the strictures of small-town life. Born to be wild, they would live like legends. Their classmates didn't have a clue. Rhonda and Dolly were hooked on their own recklessness and the sense of power that came from fearing nothing and no one. While Dolly was not quite as carefree as she made out, she was bolstered by Rhonda's example. Rhonda was too cool for words. She was already a legend.

Once they had friends with wheels, the picture theatre seemed way too tame. Clive, wearing his favourite red-checked cowboy shirt, Levi's and tooled-leather boots, his hair slicked into an Elvis lookalike style, would gun the Falcon along the beach roads out of town and do wheelies on the dirt tracks meandering off into scrub, while the girls shrieked, high on the thrill of the ride beneath wide, starry skies slung above the dark sea, stoked by the shot of vodka or Southern Comfort that kicked off the evening. This was the life!

Rhonda's father never said anything about her arriving home at dawn on Sundays. He'd be sleeping off the effects of his Saturday night at the bar of the Criterion Hotel. He hardly seemed to notice whether Rhonda was at home or not. She'd cook him dinner once in a while, but mostly they lived like strangers under the same roof. As he had with her mother. Rhonda's dad had behaved like the ghost of his former self since her mum shot through. He just wasn't with it any more. But Rhonda seldom gave this a thought. It made life easier, in a way.

Dolly's mum was a different matter. Widowed with four young children, embattled and embittered, she was chronically exhausted from working as a cleaner at the local hospital and caring for her family on her own. Although she was temperate by nature, fatigue made her lose patience, and she sometimes gave in to the impulse to rail at Dolly, calling her hurtful names out of a sense of powerlessness. She seemed to lack the authority to rein Dolly in. It would have been different if Dolly's father, a railway fettler, had not been killed in an accident on the job. Her mum was still waiting for some compensation. 'You'll come to a bad end,' she warned her daughter, 'with the company you keep! Can't you see you're putting yourself in harm's way?'

Dolly was sometimes downcast after hearing her mother's dire predictions, but then there'd be the peremptory toot of a car horn outside, and she'd be gone before her mum could say a word, cruising with Rhonda and Clive and Bruce, seduced by the ease of it all, fleeing the humdrum world where her mother eked out her days, bound for a freer space.

The boys in their class at school were out of their league with the likes of Rhonda and Dolly, though they turned longing, moon-calf eyes on the scandalous pair and resorted to name-calling to vent their frustration. Some of the girls envied the two renegades, while pretending to despise them. Nobody else they knew exuded such a palpable whiff of danger, the aura of confidence conferred by initiation into a realm their less adventurous classmates could only fantasise about. Rhonda and Dolly formed a provocatively nonchalant duo who manifestly couldn't care less what goody-two-shoes girls might say or think. They had the edge on thrills and glamour. They were having a ball.

One Saturday, Clive thought it would be a bit of a blast to take a spin up the range to a mining town on the other side. It was about seventy miles away, and the road was winding enough to be scary, which was part of the appeal. It would be a gas.

Rhonda got dressed in her sequinned denim hotpants and black suede platforms, flicking her coppery curtain of hair back over one shoulder to check her appearance in the mirror. She never wore make-up. She didn't need to. Boys and girls alike would gaze admiringly at the tiny cinnamon freckles dusting her nose and cheekbones, her mesmerising eyes that changed colour, alternating like the sea between green and blue. She was a knockout without even trying, in a black singlet and faded denim shorts with raw hems and sequinned back pockets. Her dad casually left cash lying around for clothes and food. He didn't seem to mind how she spent it. He never asked, just kept shelling out.

Dolly was more conservative. She wore her dark hair in a bob and dressed more demurely, because of her mum: a denim skirt, a red and white striped T-shirt and navy sandals. Bruce, stocky and stolid, even-tempered, was a steadier sort of guy than crazy Clive, who liked to show off. For all her efforts to match Rhonda's bravado, Dolly felt a lot safer in Bruce's hands than she did around Clive. Bruce's parents were quiet, unassuming folk, and Bruce took after them. But the boys preferred to hunt in pairs, and Clive was the one with wheels. Besides, they'd been mates since primary school, an attraction of opposites.

Off they went as the sun was setting, Clive gunning the car through the dusk, Rhonda beside him in the front, flying high on adrenalin. Clive switched on the car radio and they sang along with Elvis: 'Love Me Tender' and 'It's Now or Never', laughing as the vehicle lurched up the zigzag road to the top of the range, the passengers tossing like corks from one side to the other.

Clive lit a smoke, wound down the window and stuck his elbow out of the opening. Rhonda hooked an arm around his neck. Taking his eyes off the road for a moment, he blew hot smoke in her ear, making her squeal. He silenced her protests by giving her a puff of his cigarette, as Bruce called, 'Hey! Watch it! We nearly went off the edge just then!'

'Scared?' Clive taunted him. 'Trust me.' But he paid closer attention to the road for the rest of the way to the top.

The mining town was all lit up, and the pubs were doing a roaring trade. They stopped at a café first for burgers and chips and Pepsi, enjoying the attention reserved for strangers in town. They came in for extra scrutiny on account of Rhonda and Dolly.

'A bit under age, wouldn't y' say?' the proprietor observed, nudging the cook in the ribs with his elbow.

'Cradle snatchin' for sure,' the sweating cook agreed. 'Not our problem, though, is it?' he added, scraping onions off the hotplate.

'Oh I dunno,' said his boss. 'I could fancy a bit o' that meself. Man, could I what!'

'Get a grip,' muttered the cook. 'Jail bait for sure!'

Rhonda and Dolly went into a huddle, giggling at some private exchange. The night was just beginning, and they were intoxicated at being on the loose in this unfamiliar, gritty, masculine environment.

*

At one a.m., Rhonda's father got up and stumbled to the bathroom. Blurrily, he registered the fact that Rhonda wasn't home yet, shrugged, belched and went back to bed. Just like her mother. Never home. He felt a stab of pain in his chest, but soon dozed off again.

At two a.m., Dolly's mother woke and glanced at the clock. A sickening sense of foreboding throbbed in the pit of her stomach. Where would it end? A curlew wailed close by, making her shiver and huddle deeper under the covers. 'Please God,' she whimpered, 'don't take my daughter.' The minutes dragged. Sleep would not come.

It wasn't the first time she'd lain awake willing Dolly's return, but this time she was racked with remorse, wishing she could take back some of the unkind names she'd flung at her daughter of late…remembering how Dolly had run back inside just before leaving, to hug her tight and say, 'Don't worry, Mum, you know I love you. Don't wait up for me, I'll be OK.' Then she was gone as the car roared away.

At four a.m., two ambulances, preceded by a police car, drove at breakneck speed into the emergency bay at the local base hospital, sirens wailing, lights flashing. Two stretchers were unloaded, followed by another two.

The intern on duty turned pale when he lifted the sheet covering the face of the first casualty. 'Christ!' he said under his breath. 'Just a kid! What the hell happened out there?'

The ambulance bearer, likewise ashen faced, said in a low voice, 'When we reached the vehicle, she was hanging out of the windscreen on the driver's side. She must've been sitting in his lap as they came down the range.'

'And the others?'

Something seemed to be stuck in the paramedic's throat. His face was beginning to crumple. Then, forcing the words out, he spoke. 'I… recognise the girls. I've got a daughter…in their class. Grade seven…'

'Jesus!' said the intern. 'OK, just sign the paperwork. We'll do the rest.'

At five a.m., the phone rang in Dolly's house. Her mother was still lying sleepless, nerves strung taut with a sense of dread, waiting for her daughter to come home.

At five a.m., as day broke over the range, a crow, perched above the tangle of bloodstained metal at the foot of an ironbark, struck up his ancient, unmelodious cry. Somewhere farther away, a butcher bird burst into song – fluting, flawless, unchanged; fresh as the new dawn.

Fool's Gold

Maggie stands at her kitchen bench, staring into the distance beyond the open window above the sink. There is an insect screen on the window that blurs the clarity of what she sees. The back door to one side of the bench is open. She moves sideways to gaze vacantly through the larger screen on the doorway.

She sighs, walks through the corridor connecting the back door to the front and exits onto the front veranda. The house is on low blocks, so she cannot see beyond the mulga and gidyea scrub. A sky hazy with dust foreshortens the vertical perspective. Over to one side, a low ridge of flat-topped red rock rises above the khaki scrub. She gazes down the vehicle track that is soon swallowed up by the mulga. Al's late again. He was late last Monday too. And maybe the one before? She can't be sure now. He never used to be.

As the sun dips below the ridge Maggie hears the approaching four-wheel drive, and the battered jeep utility comes into view. She's onto her second neat whisky. She walks down the six front steps to greet him.

Al gives her shoulders a quick squeeze as he brushes past. There's a strong smell about him. It reminds her somehow of sex, but that could scarcely be the case. There isn't another woman for miles. The nearest neighbour is a widower with a son and a daughter who help run the property. She must have imagined that odour.

Al sits on the top step to pull off his boots, then follows Maggie into the kitchen.

'Yer late.'
'Yeah.'
'Food's cold.'
'Huh.'

'Thought y'must've had a flat…'
'Nah.'
'Sheep gone missing again?'
'Nope.'
'Found 'em all right then?'
'Yeah. Eventually.'
'Where?'
'West dam.'
'Thought y'were planning t'go east?'
'Yeah. Changed m'mind at the last minute…'
Crockery and cutlery clatter against wood.
'Y'd better eat then.'
'Huh.'
'Lost yer appetite?'
'I'm bushed.'
'Yer look it.'
'Yeah, well, once y'get off the track…'
'Reckon we'll be cuttin' mulga before the year's out…'

A knife and fork scrape against a plate, alternating with sounds of chewing and swallowing.

'What've y'done t'these chops?'

Maggie is perturbed by small, unaccountable changes in Al's manner. But after the meal he seems to get his second wind. He sits her on his lap like he used to when they were courting and newly wed, teasing her, making her laugh, calling her pet names, caressing the bump in her belly.

'What's my little python been swallowing this time? A whole lamb?'
She giggles, shaking her head.
'A turkey?'

She giggles still more at the thought of that bird's anatomy, and hides her face in his neck.

'Come to bed,' he says. 'I want to play with you.'
'What about the baby?'
'Trust me.'

*

The next day and the next, Maggie sings at her chores. All is right with her world. She doesn't eye the whisky bottle once.

She revisits the good times they've shared. Sunday jaunts to disused opal diggings the other side of Thargomindah. Coming home with their hats full of colours, chips and small stones with shots of paradise in their veins, as if a rainbow had used the rock as a prism, and the sun had baked the rainbow spectrum hard before it could escape.

They used to go in the winter months. In summer the heat would send you dizzy. The diggings were littered with countless shafts that lay in wait for unwary feet, echoing at a frequency beyond the range of human hearing. Echoing with ghosts of hope and despair.

On their last trip, just before her pregnancy was confirmed, they'd almost given up on finding any good pieces. There'd been lots of chips with superficial flashes of colour lying about on the arid expanse of abandoned mullock heaps, but they already had loads of those. They were always hoping for something special, but mostly finding the opaline equivalent of fool's gold. Pretty peacock stones, worth nothing.

Then she'd found it. She'd known as soon as she saw it. A pebble the size and shape of a pigeon's egg. She'd cradled it in her hand all the way home, then placed it carefully in her secret nest with several others of the same type. They'd only know the truth when the pebbles were cracked open like nuts, but she was afraid to let Al have a go at this, in case he ruined them.

Now Maggie takes down the makeshift nest from a dark corner of the kitchen dresser and counts her five eggs. They have to be worth something. They just have to be.

*

When the next Monday comes round, Al is gone again. That night he's too knocked up to eat. He goes to the shed, starts the electricity generator, then goes straight to bed.

In the morning Maggie gets up before him to inspect the jeep.

Nothing. She checks his clothes. His underwear. Can't really tell. Just body smells.

She's running out of Scotch again. Can't ask Al to get her some. He'd hit the roof. This very late pregnancy of theirs, after the three older kids have grown up and flown the coop, has taken them both by surprise, to put it mildly. Knocked the wind out of their sails. The wages of some nights and days when lust had its way. Not just lust, she reminds herself. Love was in it too. Almost like the old days, when they used to ride out on the run, inseparable, always side by side, and camp out under the stars, exhausting each other with their appetites. Now that they only had each other again, they both seemed to crave the reassurance of physical contact as proof against loneliness.

She'll ring the neighbours, she decides. Ask if they're going to town.

The neighbour's daughter, handsome, laconic, twenty-something, is at the wheel when they call by to drop off the Scotch. Al hovers in the offing, looking strangely sheepish. As Maggie reaches out to take the brown paper, bottle-shaped bag, she intercepts Al's eye contact with Jill, the driver. Maggie doesn't know the word for what she sees in the glance passing between Al and Jill, but she knows what it means.

The following Monday, as Al leaves the house, Maggie calls after him, Give my regards to Jill!

He flinches as if struck by a bullet but, pretending he hasn't heard, does not look back.

Maggie listens to the sound of the motor growing faint, placing her hand on her belly as it gives a lurch. She addresses the inmate, patting the bulge as she speaks softly, testing the words, It's you and me, Joey boy. From now on it's you and me. Let him have his fool's gold! Better start getting ready to jump…

She detects a small heartbeat, fluttering as if in response like an echo of the generator that supplies them with electricity.

With a leaden heart and mechanical hand, she extracts the frozen chops from the deep freeze. They hit the kitchen bench with a dull thud. Ice tinkles and clinks in a glass. Then there is silence. A world of silence.

None But the Lonely Heart

In my view, Alexei Nikolayich, every love, be it happy or unhappy, is a real calamity if you surrender to it entirely...

Ivan Turgenev, *A Month in the Country*

Three visitors were on their way to a house in the country for an overnight stay. Two of them were in search of some kind of illumination, although they had no idea what form this might take exactly, or whether they were even remotely likely to find it as a result of this journey. Vanya, the driver, had clear-cut expectations – modest, but specific. Galina, an acquaintance of his mother, had come from Russia to visit her sister, Lyudmila (Mila), who was married to Tom, an Australian. Tom had recently acquired a grazing property several hours drive from the provincial city where the visitors lived. Galina was the bearer of an important and confidential message from Vanya's mother, which she had promised to convey in person – verbally. What could it be that could not be entrusted to letter, email or telephone? Vanya was very anxious to find out, in fact almost ill with anticipation and apprehension. Good news? Bad news? Something intriguing?

Vanya had brought along his former wife, Alison, from whom he'd recently separated, but whom he still regarded as his closest ally. Alison, not yet reconciled to this new reality, secretly harboured hopes that the hurt and humiliation of Vanya's recent about-face might be reversed. After much urging, Vanya's friend William, a retired academic, had also been persuaded to accompany them.

Having set out at midday, the three guests did not arrive until mid-afternoon, when the winter shadows were lengthening across the empty paddocks. Mila and Galina were waiting to receive them on the front veranda of the farmhouse. They brushed cheeks with Alison, at the same time scrutinising William with some curiosity, wondering where he fitted in.

In the living room, Tom was sitting at a table with one of his neighbours, Slim, an atlas of Russia spread out before them. Both Tom and Slim were in semi-retirement on adjacent small grazing properties. Before making this move, Tom had sailed his own yacht round the world, taking Mila on as crew at one of the Baltic ports en route. Both Tom and Mila had at least half their lives behind them, although he was the elder by several years.

Mila immediately offered refreshment, while Tom, cutting across her, announced that if they were to complete his proposed tour of the property, they'd better get a move on, as it would be dark in less than two hours. Vanya had already gone into a huddle with Galina on the veranda, presumably to receive his mother's mysterious communiqué, so William, Slim and Alison climbed into the four-wheel drive. Tom growled something to Mila as the vehicle moved off. He reminded Alison of the sheriff in an old-fashioned Western movie – the same kind of broad-brimmed hat, a ginger moustache that sat on his upper lip like a shaving brush, leathery skin, riding boots, a carefully cultivated swagger. But there was no star on his chest.

The track was virtually non-existent, bone-jarringly steep and rough. The ascent was like a rodeo ride on wheels. They got out to walk the last hundred metres or so up a cone-shaped hill that commanded a three-hundred-and-sixty-degree view of the surrounding country – sun-bleached grazing land alternating with patches of dense scrub, rimmed to the west by hills and Wedgwood-blue mountains. Alison had lived on the land as a child. She sensed that these were city farmers. The property was not even stocked.

'Cattle cost too much now,' Tom told her, adding, however, that the entire shire abounded in wild deer, descendants of stock Queen Victoria presented to the district in colonial times.

Back at the house, there was one more visitor – a younger man with soulful brown eyes, a softer personality than Tom; a little shy, perhaps, like Slim. His name was Colin. He could not conceal his interest in Galina. He kept gazing at her like a boy at a cake-shop window.

Under the veranda in a cloud of smoke, Mila was tending the barbecue. Her features were set in a wooden expression bespeaking stoicism and private misery. Alison guessed that Tom was not an easy man to live with. The set of his features indicated a cruel streak, and the seemingly gratuitous description of his part in a neighbour's recent branding-castrating-earmarking of Charolais cattle more or less confirmed it. She remembered such talk from her childhood. Then, she had come to realise that when men speak in the presence of females about castrating animals, this is somehow meant to convey a message about their own virility. Such talk had always sickened her, along with the act it evoked. Mila reminded her of a horse that had been maltreated by an unfeeling owner, and suffered in silence because it had no means of expressing its despair.

Before the food was served, Alison, William and Slim sat out on the veranda next to a powerful telescope, through which they took turns looking at Venus, smouldering low in the sky near a crescent moon. The planet burned like an acetylene flare, as enigmatic and remote when viewed through the lens as with the naked eye. It seemed to embody the inaccessible and unattainable, accentuating the underlying joylessness of the occasion. From somewhere near the dark treeline, a dingo was howling to the moon. Alison fancied the wild dog's cry sounded similar to that of wolves.

She struck up a conversation with Tom's neighbour, Slim – a lonely, kind, shy-hearted man, she sensed, who had brought along his little dog, Buffy. Observing Buffy and Slim, Alison reflected that the pet's personality was very likely a canine version of the man's: diffident, polite, not wishing to impose. She noticed this when she fetched a bowl of water to offer the animal. Buffy was thirsty, but waited for permission and reassurance before accepting the water, then drank almost apologetically. Slim was like certain gentle rural bachelors of Alison's past – bashful, modest men who would never hurt a fly. She wondered what Slim and Tom had in common, and why Mila was with Tom and not Slim, who would surely be kinder to her, and more appreciative. Surprisingly, Slim had travelled abroad quite a lot, mainly in Asia and the Pacific.

Mila appeared with platters of barbecued meat and salad. 'Slim was in navy,' she volunteered.

Alison warmed to Slim. He was reminiscent of a minor character in the films shown at Saturday matinees she was sometimes taken to as a child – men from a world of small towns and defined horizons, shaped by different values from those that had now come to the fore. 'Don't romanticise people,' she told herself crossly. Slim hungered for human companionship. He was definitely subordinate in personality to Tom. Perhaps they'd met in the navy? She wondered why two seafaring men would choose to settle in this landlocked place, so far removed from their accustomed element.

Mila sat to one side with her lapdog, a bright-eyed bundle of fluff with no teeth, recently rescued, as Mila explained, from a situation of near-fatal neglect, where it had wasted away to skin and bone. As Mila sat fondling her pet, feeding it morsels of food that didn't require chewing, her features relaxed and softened. It was the only time during the visit when she seemed at peace.

Colin sat next to Galina, devouring her with his eyes. She was slender and tense, attractive in a rather distant way. In Russia she worked as a meteorologist. They didn't talk directly to each other, but Galina chattered incessantly while Vanya interpreted, trying to keep up. Galina kept switching topics, although her general theme was culture shock. First of all, names. When Australians talked to each other, they didn't use first names, but addressed their remarks instead to an impersonal, implied 'you'. In Russia, this would be considered demeaning, or at best off-hand. And yet it was the opposite with endearments, which elsewhere implied familiarity. Why did Australians use these so casually? They didn't use names when they'd been introduced, yet they said 'love' and 'darl' to complete strangers.

Social invitations were another sticking point. If a man invited a woman to dine with him in Russia, he wouldn't dream of expecting her to pay for her meal. And speaking of money, why were Australians so stingy? Why did husbands and wives keep separate bank accounts, saying 'This is mine, that's yours'? Many forms of behaviour here, especially of men towards women, would be regarded as showing a lack of respect in Russia. She had the impression that the folk she had met so far didn't seem aware of, or sensitive to, others' feelings.

Colin listened and looked. He didn't seem to mind Galina's implied criticisms. He was clearly smitten, already dreaming of her beside him at the altar, 'tying the knot' as the wedding bells pealed.

Vanya got sidetracked by Mila in a discussion about the existence of God.

Tom said, 'Oh, for Christ's sake! Will you listen to this?'

William went out to look at the stars. He wasn't sure why he was there, or what to make of those people. It all seemed a far cry from what he had read in Turgenev and Chekhov.

Alison gazed at the setting moon. Five years ago, in a faraway country, she and Vanya had spent their first night together, and her world had been spun into a different part of the galaxy. Not by the physical event so much as the meeting of different planets that nonetheless emitted weirdly compatible frequencies. Or so she had thought. She knew she was present now only for moral support, which Vanya no longer seemed to need.

*

The discussion about God had become deadlocked. Mila was stubborn as a mule. If there was no empirical proof of God's existence, then there was no God, she insisted. Vanya would make no concessions. God was an act of faith, he contended. Proof? demanded Mila. Faith, insisted Vanya. What proof did Mila have that there was no God? Both of them turned on Alison, who soon felt trapped – between cultures, languages, viewpoints. She pleaded a headache and, knowing it was socially inappropriate in the eyes of all present, said she'd better be off to bed.

'There is no God!' bawled Tom from in front of the TV, where he and Slim were watching the footy.

Slim excused himself on the grounds that he had an early start the next day – April 25th. Dawn ceremonies would be held at war memorials throughout the land. Slim, having seen service in the navy, was bound to honour that tradition. He was the only one not staying the night.

Alison took the bundle of bedding Mila fished out of the linen closet. The guest room under the house contained two single beds, the second of which was intended for William. Vanya had grabbed a sleeping bag, although he was clearly not planning to sleep for a while yet.

Resenting the way Vanya had manoeuvred her into sharing a room with a virtual stranger, Alison quickly got into bed, wanting to fall asleep before William retired, to spare them both embarrassment. William was seventy-five, and certainly not the importunate type, but the sleeping arrangement nevertheless struck her as odd, to say the least. As it was, she woke several times to hear debate raging overhead, and William, who was getting over a cold, snuffling in his sleep.

The next morning, Tom and Mila, Colin and Galina were still asleep when Alison, Vanya and William made their way to the kitchen, where the table was set for breakfast with bread, cheese, and various spreads. Coffee and tea had been left out on the bench. Vanya claimed not to have slept at all, William said he'd slept very badly, and Alison was still simmering with resentment at having to sleep under the scrutiny of a man she did not feel comfortable with. Although it was illogical under the circumstances, it felt like a betrayal. Vanya should have been there to protect her.

Colin and Galina appeared separately, Colin looking sheepish and unshaven, Galina characteristically cool and smartly dressed. Eventually Mila emerged, her face more woodenly miserable than ever, and volunteered without enthusiasm to cook bacon and eggs. William and Colin, seeming not to notice her leaden expression, eagerly accepted the offer.

Vanya, Galina and Alison went down to the yard and chatted, waiting for the others to join them in a walk across the empty pastures. There was, albeit incongruously, some mention made of Pushkin. Alison confessed that her favourite part of *Eugene Onegin* was Tatyana's letter – not so much for its content as for the way Pushkin had managed to capture a young girl's innocent voice, her inflections.

Galina was scathing. 'That kind of romanticism is not only unrealistic, but also very harmful,' she declared, adding darkly, 'Pushkin has a lot to answer for!'

There was a light cloud cover and a Sunday-morning hush in the air when they set off across the paddocks, the farm dog bounding ahead of them. The grass was still wet with dew.

'It's the first time I've missed the Anzac dawn service,' said Colin.

Alison glanced at him sharply. Was he a veteran too? He was far too young to have served in Vietnam. Maybe East Timor? Iraq? But he didn't seem to mind this break with tradition. Contemplating their little company straggling along the overgrown path, her thoughts began to drift in William's mental footsteps of the previous day. Turgenev. Chekhov. She'd seen films based on some of their plays; had read some of their stories.

The ramble through the morning paddocks to a sombre, stagnant, almost sinister lagoon, complete with lily pads and heron, but no actual water lilies, was not unlike a house party on a Russian provincial estate. If this were a play or a story by Chekhov or Turgenev, they'd all return to the house and drink tea and philosophise in a desultory way, and perhaps someone would find a quiet corner to read or write in a diary before setting off on a picnic, or in search of berries and mushrooms… there'd be more activity in the kitchen, but Mila would organise servants to do the work, and there'd be those melancholy undercurrents of unrequited love, with the afflicted parties in denial of their loveless fate. But the analogy with scenes from Turgenev and Chekhov didn't really apply – it was all too tenuous, fractured…

Vanya had realised afresh that he couldn't commit himself emotionally, couldn't risk himself in love, and besides, found philosophy and art far more rewarding than personal relationships. Consciously or otherwise, he embodied the attitude familiar to readers of Turgenev that every love, happy as well as unhappy, is a real calamity when you surrender to it entirely, so he kept his romantic impulses in check at all times. Galina, also wary, was nevertheless quite attracted to Vanya, in a distracted, abstract kind of way. Colin was more doggedly determined than ever to attempt the impossible – winning Galina's heart, which was closed to him. Alison ruefully acknowledged defeat in love at Vanya's hands, but was not yet able or willing to untie the knot of their storm-tossed friendship, one strand of which had loosened and partly unravelled, while another had become more convoluted than ever. The associations that linked them seemed dense and impenetrable to outsiders, almost like blood ties.

William's dead wife was never far from his thoughts, her imagined presence his anchor and anchorage in life. Slim, perhaps still present in spirit, was standing to attention in front of some lonely, small-town cenotaph, quietly wondering why Tom could not show any tenderness to Lyudmila. Mila's mutiny had hardened to something adamantine, which Tom was equally determined to crush, to show himself and her who was boss.

Back at the house, they were probably facing off over breakfast, as she sullenly scorched another serving of bacon and eggs. Mila, a scientist, had no liking for, or patience with, cooking. Tom's daily expectations chafed. Her psyche was a mass of saddle galls. It was no accident that he'd brought her to the depths of the country. If he couldn't subdue her spirit, he'd bury her alive.

The walking party returned to the house. Only Colin stayed for morning tea. As they drove away, Vanya related how he'd spent the night interpreting for Colin and Galina, who'd confided to him that Colin had offended her mortally by inviting her to dinner and then expecting her to pay for her meal, by not addressing her by name (which he apparently could not pronounce), by buying a sandwich for himself and not offering one to her – he had lost her before he was ever in any position to win her. By coincidence, however, they'd both had near-death experiences, at almost the same time, in almost the same circumstances, which they described in almost the same imagery.

Galina had already been married and divorced three times. All her husbands, she conceded, had been good men – non-drinkers, non-smokers, and strictly monogamous. Their only shortcoming had been the fact that she had not found them romantic enough.

*

The momentous news from Vanya's mother had turned out to be anti-climactic – something about her plans to separate from her current spouse. Vanya found it difficult to register this as feeling. Taking one hand off the steering wheel, he patted himself on the chest and ribs a few times as if checking for bruises. Nothing.

At a point when the silence in the car began to seem oppressive, Vanya started to hum under his breath, then to warble a few bars, like an opera singer warming up.

Нет, только тот, кто знал	No, only one who's known
Свиданья жажду,	The thirst for meeting
Поймёт, как я страдал	Will realise how I've suffered
И как я стражду.	And shall suffer…

'What's that you're singing?' Alison asked, eager as ever to be included in his world, and forgetting for the moment that she'd been relegated to a lesser role.

'Chaikovsky,' came the curt rejoinder.

'I don't recognise it.'

'None but the lonely heart,' he said, irritation in his tone, then, abruptly changing tack, 'Does anyone want to stop for coffee?'

'Not I,' said William.

'Not really,' said Alison.

Vanya shrugged, accelerating slightly. An unbroken silence ensued until they pulled up outside William's house.

William was most relieved to arrive home. He walked down the garden path, unlocked his front door, waved to Vanya and Alison, stepped over the threshold, then closed the door to the outside world firmly behind him. He would have much to relate when next he received a longed-for visitation from his dear, departed wife. Perhaps she would be able to make some sense of all this nonsense.

Poor Blighter

People said at first it was the loneliness that got to him, then the drink. They said it might have been different if his parents hadn't retired from the farm, leaving him the sole occupant of the old weatherboard farmhouse. After they died it was worse. Harder to bear, then intolerable. Franz could no longer imagine that one day they might return, bringing back the bonhomie of former times, coaxing the appetising whiff of cinnamon and yeast from an oven that had been neither used nor cleaned in more than a decade. More and more, he missed the cheerful bustle of mealtimes with aromas of food from the old country: pork roasting with apple and caraway seeds; sauerkraut, *Kartoffelsuppe*. He'd never managed to cook those dishes the way his mother had. When he'd tried, they didn't taste the same. Cooking was women's work.

People said it might have been different if he'd been more outgoing, but he was a reclusive type, except with his own countryfolk. Franz had been an adolescent when they arrived from war-shattered Europe, old enough to remember the war and his homeland in ruins, too old to make the transition to schooling in a foreign language. He had attended school for only a couple of years, excluded from learning by his incomprehension of English, then left as soon as he turned fourteen, the legal school leaving age, with a sense of deliverance from a grotesque ordeal.

Ten good years had followed, working the farm with his father, socialising with their compatriots, who formed a lively enclave in the small coastal community. The weekend gatherings lit up the workdays to come with their camaraderie, anecdotes, singing, dancing and hearty home-cooked fare, liberally accompanied by wine and beer. Even there, he was never at the centre of activity. The other teenagers from their social set seemed to share an ease of association that Franz didn't feel, but he never felt excluded, either. Mostly he was content to look on, eat, drink, perhaps dance a little when things warmed up, and bask in the general glow.

His family were farming folk from the periphery of the former state they had fled after Hitler's defeat, and somehow Franz personified this marginal status. Unlike the once-vaunted Aryan prototype, Franz and his parents and sister were stocky with dark hair and eyes, more like Gypsies than Teutons in appearance, which was not uncommon for the region they hailed from. People in his own community said among themselves it was a pity his squint marred an otherwise good-looking face, lending it a rakish, slightly villainous cast. As he never confided his thoughts or feelings, nobody could tell how much this bothered him. But it marked him and set him apart from his peers, who were perfect physical specimens despite the war. They all had strong, straight bones, perfect teeth and complexions, flaxen hair, whereas he was swarthy and thickset, like many of the people of his borderland province.

Despite the vitality of their immigrant enclave, a strange phenomenon had occurred whereby within a couple of decades of their arrival in the farming settlement after their initial stint in the northern canefields, almost the entire community was on the move again. It was uncharacteristic behaviour for farmers, but the war had taught them that nothing is permanent, and their industry had given them the means to retire to places of their own choosing, so many left the district and moved to other, distant townships settled by earlier generations of their compatriots and bearing place names from their homeland. Franz was one of the few who remained.

People said it might have been different if he'd met the right girl. They weren't to know that he *had* met the right girl – right for him, that is – but he had not been right for her. She liked him well enough, they danced together like a dream, but she was looking for something else: a farmer's daughter who had sworn not to become a farmer's wife. The romantic interlude was over within months, never to be repeated.

After that, there seemed to be no star to pin his dream to, and the only girls he had occasional dealings with were the wrong girls – the kind he could never tell his mother about, or introduce to his family. Or marry.

The farm became a burden. It was too much for one man to manage, so he had to hire day labourers when he could find them. The pineapples were seasonal, which made it easier, but the other crops needed more constant attention, and motivation waned. Who was he doing this for? His parents were gone, they didn't need his labour. They didn't need anything anymore. His sister, the only sibling, was married and lived far away. He had no prospects of marriage or a family. There didn't seem much point. That was when the alcohol began to take over.

Franz was able to conceal this fact for a time, even from himself. After all, he was still young and strong, tempered by the years of rigorous physical work and able to withstand the depredations of liquor. But then the telltale signs began to appear. Normally clean-shaven and presentably attired, he was seen in the opposite state. He neglected to eat properly, becoming a less frequent diner at the small café on the edge of town that served good home-cooked meals.

Pat, the proprietor, concerned for his welfare, tried to engage him in conversation when he reappeared. 'How have you been, love? We haven't seen you in a while. I've been worried about you.'

But Franz only regarded her stolidly with his one good eye as he kept forking roast potato into his mouth.

'Well,' Pat continued, 'you know that if you ever need anything, you only have to ask, love.'

If only he could! But Franz had never learned to ask. It was neither in his culture or conditioning, nor in his nature to do so.

It seemed that the only creature to whom he could show tenderness was his hunting dog, Mitzi; and hunting became his solitary, savage pleasure. Mostly wallabies, which he skinned, feeding their flesh to Mitzi. It helped to get him away from the bottle, which he now regarded with loathing, but always returned to at the end of the day.

People were starting to speculate about him. Yet for all their talk, which was not malicious, no one knew how to approach him or what they could do. A neighbour, nagged by the thought that the poor blighter on the next farm must be lonely and may be in some kind of trouble, finally resolved to bite the bullet and go to Franz to see if he could do anything to help. But his own farm kept him busy, so he found excuses to postpone the visit.

One Saturday evening, Franz showered, shaved, donned his Sunday suit, slicked down his hair, splashed *Kölnisch Wasser* on his smooth cheeks, took out the old gramophone records his parents had left behind, and played the familiar songs and dances to the accompaniment of a good bottle of schnapps, cheese, wurst and rye bread, like in the old days when his parents were alive and still on the farm. He spread out the photographs of those times: the young, glowing faces, hope in their eyes.

There was one of his prospective bride, the farmer's daughter who'd fled rural life. He remembered the soft voile forget-me-not-blue dress she'd worn that summer, the way it matched her eyes. He remembered lying on the grass with his head in her lap, gazing up at those unforgettable eyes, the same colour as the cloudless sky that day, and thinking he had never been so happy. Just before she'd left for the city she'd kissed him, half tearful, half laughing, farewelling him with just one word: *Vergissmeinnicht*. Forget-me-not. He had never forgotten her for a moment, but she'd given no sign that she remembered him. Where was she now? He'd never heard from her again. He felt cheated by her prejudice. They'd had such good times. If he weren't a farmer, they might still be together.

Franz studied all the images soberly, for a long time. The more schnapps he imbibed, the clearer his head became. He switched on every light in the house and sat for a while, considering. Opening the drawer of the kitchen dresser, he took out his father's old Luger pistol, checking to see if it was loaded.

The phone rang. Who could it be, on a Saturday night? Perhaps his sister. He ignored it. Moving through the silent rooms, he took deliberate and careful aim at each of the lights and heard them shatter. Without shades, the naked bulbs made easy targets. The phone rang again, but he scarcely noticed. Mitzi began to howl. She howled all night and into the next day, until finally the neighbours came to investigate.

The Agency of Love

Quatrefoil

💮 Praise Be

– Are you ever coming back?

– Back where?

– To the farm.

– No.

He hung his head, the hat in his hand half covering his chest like a mourner at a graveside. She continued peeling potatoes and paring the rind off pumpkin, rearranging the chopping board and knife with inordinate care. The man stood behind her like a chastised boy.

– What about Dad?

– What about him?

A potato made a crisp sound like a ricochet as she split it in two with the knife. Starch was whitening the surface of the board.

– We can't leave him there by himself.

– Why not?

He did not reply. The reasons were self-evident.

– He won't be lonely, she added in a toneless voice, with you for company.

He swallowed. Swallowing his pride.

She turned and glanced at him as if he'd just arrived. He looked like a boy who'd lost his mother. One half of her heart melted while the other half turned to stone. Yet there was no mistaking the hurt in his face, the bewilderment. The farm had sapped her vitality, along with her father-in-law and husband, who now stood before her like a supplicant; not to mention the tribe of children the latter had bestowed on her. Now, not for the first time, she realised that this husband of hers, from whom she needed a complete break, was the neediest of all.

But surely she'd done enough? For the first time since her marriage, she had a little money of her own. Hard-earned money, wages from cleaning other people's houses. Just enough to make her mistress of this rented cottage. Her own space.

– Sit down, she said. You're making the place look untidy.

Obediently, he sat. She handed him a cup of tea. Why were men so helpless? Would there ever be an end to this?

– I suppose I'd better be going, he said, finishing the tea.

– Suit yourself.

– Can I give you a hand with anything?

– Not really.

– I'd better get back to Dad, then.

She handed him a bundle wrapped in a clean tea towel. It smelt savoury: mixed herbs and meat.

– Rissoles and jacket-baked potatoes, she said in her most apathetic tone.

His eyes filled with gratitude. Like a dog's, she thought, embarrassed for him.

*

An hour and a half later, she heard the farm utility pull up outside. Without taking her eyes from the television screen, she heard him come in. He placed a basket beside her chair. In it were some freshly-picked beans, new-laid eggs, passionfruit and, unexpectedly, a large, red, voluptuous hibiscus.

He shuffled his feet like a schoolboy waiting outside the principal's office.

– Dad said thank you for the dinner.

A minute or so elapsed.

– Car's been playing up. There's something wrong with the carburettor. Not sure whether it'll get me home…

– Have you eaten?

She spoke as if she hadn't heard a word he'd said.

– I left the food for Dad.

– Sit down then.

She placed a serving of potato and pumpkin and chops in front of him. He ate in silence, then rose to go.

– Thank you. That hit the spot. Well, I guess I'd better be making tracks.

– What about the carburettor?

He looked sheepish.

– I don't suppose you'd let me stay till it gets light…

The hint of a smile twitched at the corners of her lips, but in his anxiety he didn't notice it.

– I might. Just this once. The bed's made up in the spare room.

His heart sang like a choirboy. Praise be.

🌡 For Her Own Good

The dog sensed that something was amiss, or afoot, though seemingly the old woman didn't. The dog was uneasy for them both, and shadowed Sarah so closely as she moved about the house that she almost tripped over him. She scolded him, and he cringed at her tone, but continued to get underfoot, staying close so they couldn't be separated, to protect her.

Marlene, the youngest daughter, who had arrived un-announced the previous day, cleared the breakfast bowls and mugs with mechanical cheerfulness, as was her way. Her mother was getting ready to go to the doctor. The receptionist had called first thing that morning and asked her to come for a check-up. It was unusual to get an appointment at such short notice, and in fact Sarah couldn't recall having requested one, but she was of a generation that trusted doctors implicitly.

A taxi bore Sarah and Marlene away. In the yard, the dog whimpered, fretting. They returned an hour later in a different vehicle, with Sarah's middle daughter, Bertha, and her husband. Bertha wanted Sarah to sign a form relinquishing the dog.

The dog waited for Sarah to open the back door, but Marlene blocked the way. Bertha said there was no time now. Although they had told Sarah practically nothing, so as not to confuse or upset her, they were anxious to leave, as the place they had selected for their mother to spend the rest of her life was far away. Her refusal to cooperate was slowing them down. Peevishly Bertha explained again that once the forms were signed, the dog could go to a good home. Otherwise, there was no guarantee.

Sarah was assailed by voices telling her it was for her own good. This phrase had been ringing in her ears since Bertha appeared at the doctor's surgery, armed with documents Sarah had signed just weeks before, appointing Bertha her sole guardian with enduring power of attorney. This had also been for the best, as the solicitor had stressed, commending Sarah on her prudent decision. Now other documents had been added by the doctor, also for her own good. Sarah had trusted them all, until now.

No alarm bells had rung when Marlene arrived. The ideal person to smooth the way, she was like the reliable horse kept at an abattoir to lead the other animals to slaughter. Not that those present were thinking in such terms. Rather, they were congratulating themselves that all was going according to plan. By the next day their mother would be ensconced in the aged care facility they had selected, unbeknownst to her, in a place she had never seen before.

Sarah could not take in what was happening. It made no sense. As she was led to the car, the dog thrust his muzzle under the gate, straining for a last whiff of the familiar, reassuring scent that pervaded the house along with his own. Only Marlene remained there now, making urgent phone calls, cancelling Meals on Wheels and other services. He knew she would not let him in. Marlene left on the evening train. The dog had already been taken away.

The next day a box sent by post was delivered to Sarah's front door, the weekly consignment of groceries from her other daughter, Claire, as yet unaware of her mother's fate. The sender awaited a call, the pleasure of knowing the box had arrived.

The box smelt of coffee and apples, but as summer ramped up the heat, the fresh fruit aroma began to ferment. The phone had been disconnected, along with the patterns and rhythms of Sarah's life. Somewhere, a thousand miles away, strangers were serving her three meals a day.

Now when Sarah woke in the night and reached out a hand in the darkness to touch the familiar coarse coat and be reassured by the lick of a warm tongue, her fingers encountered emptiness. There was not a day went by when Sarah didn't think about her dog and wonder where he was, hoping he was loved and fed and given shelter. Yet she really couldn't imagine him anywhere other than the place she'd called home. He was so staunchly loyal and protective that he'd trusted nobody but her.

Marlene and Bertha detested the dog, resenting the affection their mother lavished on him. They noticed the scuffed furniture and recoiled from the canine smell in the carpet. Where does all that love go, Sarah wondered. Is there somewhere in the animal that it can be stored, like voltage in batteries, to tide a creature over leaner seasons?

Sarah couldn't imagine where her dog might be now. Her daughters hadn't mentioned him, and she knew better than to ask. One thing she was sure of: for as long as he had breath in his body, he had not forgotten her.

Bertha, who had arranged Sarah's extradition and the disposal of her dog, and Marlene, who had helped carry out the plan, agreed they should never allude to the past in Sarah's presence, as it would only confuse her, and she probably wouldn't remember any of it anyway.

♥ A Smile to Die For

Was it the aromas of freshly baked bread, vanilla and cinnamon that enticed them to the bakery, or the girl serving customers? They draped themselves over the plate-glass counter, bees to honeycomb.

'Keep the change, honey.'

'Give us a smile!'

'How's about a date?'

'Gee you're purty, what's ya name?'

'Hey, don't make the lady blush!'

'A smahl t' dah fur!'

Heartfelt sighs and chuckles subsided abruptly as Mrs B. emerged from behind the curtain screening the shop from the bakery.

'You boys being served?' she would inquire, pleasant but crisp.

'Yes'm.'

'Yes, *mam*!'

Munching their pies and lamingtons and sticky buns, rustling tissue paper and crackling paper bags, they would leave reluctantly, with many a wink and a wave and a backward glance.

'See ya soon, honey.'

'They had such funny accents,' she recalls, shaking her head in amusement. 'They came from all over, but didn't know where they were bound for…'

'Did you ever go out with any of them?'

'Oh no!' A vehement shake of the head.

'You were waiting for Jimmy, right?'

A scarcely perceptible nod; a silence.

'We were expecting an invasion. Darwin was bombed, midget subs were sighted in coastal waters, the *Centaur* was sunk just east of Brisbane… We never saw those boys again, once they left our town. But I still remember some of their names, and where they were from…'

'You and your mum were alone at that time, weren't you?'

'There was a rifle at home, one of Dad's. One day I took it and asked to join the rifle club. We all lived from day to day. There was this nervous energy in the air, an atmosphere of fear and sometimes fragile gaiety. At the same time we knew we had to be patient, to wait for it all to play out. We didn't talk about the fear, but it was always there. Fear for ourselves and for those away in the jungles and deserts, defending us.

And there was this other feeling I've had from time to time ever since the war – it was a kind of nostalgia for a future we might not live to see…that many of those soldiers knew they would never see. They lived from moment to moment, from smile to smile… '

'So you joined the rifle club as self-defence?'

'To protect my mum. I was the only girl at the range, the first who'd ever been allowed to join, in fact, but the older men at the club were kind to me. The young men were all away at the war.'

She catches my fleeting smile and bridles slightly. 'Do you find it amusing, that I was the only girl?'

'No, I think you were incredibly brave and resourceful.' My smile had been one of involuntary admiration, not amusement. I try to imagine her aged eighteen, armed with an old rifle, preparing to hold off an invasion force threatening her town and her home.

There are tears in the old woman's eyes. 'I wish I could bring them all back,' she murmurs. 'Those boys from Wisconsin and Oklahoma… Ohio, Illinois…chiacking and ordering pies when they weren't even hungry. Just for a smile. They'd do anything for a smile. How I wish I could bring back the lads from our town and our farms – back from the deserts and jungles, the burning planes…' Her voice falters, then adds almost inaudibly, 'and Jimmy… If only I could see Jimmy, home on leave, just one more time…'

Jimmy was a survivor of the long and bitter campaign at Tobruk, with whom she'd been briefly reunited before his redeployment to New Guinea. The love of her young life, the impact of his death would ricochet through all her days and nights: waste and loss and pity, the residue of pre-war joy; the burden of remembering – the one thing she could do for him. She had, in a sense, remained a prisoner of the war that for him had long since ended.

Farther along the corridor a bell rings for afternoon tea. Sunrays brushed with gleams of honey find her westward-facing window. For a few moments her face seems smoother, younger. Her eyes brighten. Contemplating times and places, people I can't see, they emanate the light of youth that lured those uniformed boys to the bakery. The ghost of a smile I've never seen plays about her lips as she recalls their banter, their clumsy overtures and naive goodwill: 'a smahl t'dah fur'…

❦ Furlough

> Our soul is escaped even as a bird out of the snare of the fowlers: the snare is broken and we are delivered.
>
> Psalms 124:7

As Rose looked up from her crochet, her gaze froze. There at the garden gate was the person she'd been waiting for.

'Patrick!' She leapt to her feet, dropping her half-finished d'oyley, and was running down the path in an instant.

Patrick was wearing his uniform and his officer's cap, as he had been the last time she'd seen him. 'Rose,' he said quietly.

His face was grey with fatigue, she noticed.

'Come on, I don't have long. Just time enough for that brief honeymoon I promised you. Remember?'

From habit, the fingers of her right hand strayed to the ring on her left one, as if for verification, or to check that the ring had not somehow slipped off.

'I'll get my things,' she said breathlessly, 'and change into my going-away dress.'

'There's no time for that, Rose,' he said in a voice she scarcely recognised. But then, how long had it been since the wedding? 'Just come as you are,' he said more gently. 'You know you always look lovely to me.'

He took her hand in his, and she was struck by the coldness of his palm, but before she could wonder at that, she was chilled by a gust of wind rushing past her ears.

Then they were standing before the entrance of an imposing building whose portico was guarded by a pair of bronze lions.

'Is this a hotel?' she asked timidly.

'No, my love,' he said. 'Come in, I want to show you something.'

Inexplicably, she found herself ensconced in a chair at a hospital bedside. The patient in the bed was none other than Patrick, and she was sitting with his hand clasped in both of hers. His brow was clammy with fever, and she was afraid to lift the coverlet, which was arranged over a frame so as not to put pressure on his torso and lower limbs. She realised he must have been wounded, but shied away from sighting the proof. In fact, she remembered receiving the news. Messines Ridge: the words came back to haunt her afresh.

'Messines Ridge,' she said aloud, and again, abruptly the scene changed. This could not possibly be the honeymoon destination. She thought she'd be deafened by the din of explosions, and in the intervals between, the screams of mortal agony. There was a stench that made her want to retch, and she could not see Patrick. Looking down at her hand, she saw she was still wearing her wedding ring.

'Rose!' She heard his voice now, through a pall of smoke. 'This way! We must go back.'

Now they were in a chapel that she recognised from their wedding day. Lilies everywhere. More like a funeral, came the unbidden thought, as quickly suppressed. Patrick was at her side, in uniform. He'd been given forty-eight hours furlough.

'…to have and to hold, from this day forward, for better, for worse, for richer, for poorer, in sickness and in health, to love and to cherish, till death do us part. And hereto I plight you my troth,' intoned the clergyman.

Patrick's voice was strangely muffled, and her own sounded as if it were travelling along a tunnel, or a trench – coming from afar. Then Patrick was placing the ring on her finger, which was disconcerting, as moments ago she had seen it with her own eyes, already there…

'Now for that honeymoon I promised you,' her bridegroom was saying with a quixotic smile. 'Though it will not be as we had hoped, I fear…'

Minutes later, the duty nurse found Rose slumped in her chair on the veranda, the half-finished d'oyley on the floor beside her.

'She looked at peace,' the nurse reported to her supervisor. 'But then they usually do, don't they? Especially when there's been no acute illness, or pain. A merciful release, really.'

How could the staff at the nursing home ever have guessed the last words Rose had heard Patrick speak?

'Rose, my Rose of all the world, the flesh is very beautiful when we are young and undefiled by war or the ravages of ageing, but it can never be more beautiful than the spirit that stays luminous, the steadfast love illumining a life, that never fades…'

Vergissmeinnicht

for Anni

🌼 Frau Krüger Meets a Monster

Frau Krüger picked her way among the giant tree ferns along the lip of the gully, marvelling at the magnitude and grace of their fronds. There was no water in the gully, yet there must have been enough moisture to sustain them, for they continued to unfurl in fuzzy whorls tinged with a hint of copper, reminding her of the scroll on violins and cellos. Some of them were tall enough for her to stand beneath.

It was unusually fresh and cool for a summer morning. Filtered through chlorophyll, the air wafted astringent scents of bushland. She felt revived by the abundant, still unaccustomed loveliness. Behind her the mountain rose above her new home – a farm bought jointly with another *Heimat* family, with the proceeds of several seasons cutting cane (the men) and picking tobacco then stringing the leaves for drying (their wives). There was no cane-growing here in the Capricornia hinterland – just pineapples and pawpaws, market vegetables, mangoes and strawberries.

Frau Krüger had ventured to the gully in some trepidation, on the suspicion that Helga, her speckled hen, was nesting there. She'd observed Helga sidling in that direction, secretive yet purposeful. This time she had followed the hen, but lost sight of her in the bracken lining the gully's sides. Farther down were lantana thickets, but there'd be no chance of penetrating those.

Trudi, her fox terrier cross, trotted ahead of Frau Krüger. Trudi was a fearless little thing, keen-eyed and alert to any perceived threat or intruder. Now, without warning, the dog stopped in her tracks. Frau

Krüger gasped. Above the lip of the gully reared a monstrous head, bigger than Trudi's. *Gott im Himmel!* What was it? Must be a giant lizard. A…goanna. She gave a sharp cry of warning. Trudi! *Komm her!*

But Trudi was already springing at the brute's throat. Frau Krüger watched in helpless horror as the goanna thrashed to and fro with Trudi hanging on for grim death, her teeth sunk into its neck. Seeing blood on Trudi's head and chest, she ran forward wildly, flapping her apron and shrieking her pet's name, alternating with invective intended to repulse the goanna.

Hearing her screams, her husband, Urs, dropped his hoe and came running from the cultivation. Frau Krüger meanwhile became hysterical. Images were crisscrossing her inner horizon like tracers. Two men – a Russian and a German – she had witnessed in hand to hand combat in her family's barn as the tide of war turned. The German boy was Hitler Youth, a stripling. The Russian was an older man with grey in his unkempt beard and hair. The boy was armed with a pitchfork, his adversary with a bayonet. In just such horror she had watched their duel to the death from the hayloft, unable to give vent to the excruciating suspense and fear, choking back panic.

Now she could not restrain herself. Howls of protest gushed from the pit of her stomach to issue from her throat.

Nein, Trudi, *nein, nein!* she shrieked. *Nein! Du musst nicht!*

Once again she tasted the bile of her own powerlessness. Seizing a piece of dead branch from the ground she rushed forward again, but could not strike the writhing, thrashing, interlocked bodies for fear of missing her aim and harming Trudi.

Through the miasma of confused sensations and emotions, half demented with fear, she heard the thud of running footsteps. Another soldier! Friend or foe? But it was Urs whose face came into focus. Sobbing, she collapsed into his arms.

A week before, she had been skirting the cultivation when the earth in her peripheral vision seemed to move. Before her startled gaze something reared up from it. A leathery fan snapped open around an iguana face, from which a tongue flicked out at her. Frau Krüger had fled shrieking to the farmhouse, too terrified even to glance behind to see if the grotesque creature was in pursuit. The men had laughed at her then, and gone to see for themselves. Nothing, they said. A woman's imagination. Now they'd have to believe her.

At this point, Frau Krüger's overwhelmed consciousness came farther adrift from its physical surroundings. Across her mind flashed scenes from her childhood, as if she had fallen out of the present time and place, propelled by panic, into a distant realm where she'd felt safe, a ten-year-old girl on her family's farm in north-western Pomerania, close to the Baltic: an idyllic childhood, insulated against threat or strife.

The rhythms of her family life were reassuring in their sense of purpose. Her parents cultivated oats and rye, the best potatoes she had ever tasted, and flax for spinning into thread and weaving into linen. All their clothes and household linen were homespun, of the finest quality, beautifully detailed and figured with drawn threadwork and embroidery.

Every afternoon throughout primary school (before she was sent away to boarding school), wearing pinafores and leather boots, Liesl and her sister would hurry home to help in the house. The best times were watching her mother baking bread and cakes, or preserving fruit and vegetables in the summer and autumn. Their industrious, skilful mother taught her daughters to spin and weave, to knit and sew and embroider. Her family had a proud tradition of skilled needlework.

On Sundays Liesl's family attended the Lutheran church in the village, and, as it was forbidden to work on the Sabbath, she and her sisters were free to spend Sunday afternoons as they pleased. Sometimes they made dolls from corn cobs, whose silken tassels became tresses of hair. They fashioned features from beads and bright seeds, and sewed clothes from scraps of fabric. In autumn they collected chestnut and walnut shells to make miniature dolls' furniture.

And there was a startling, sky-blue memory. What was that? Ah yes! The forget-me-nots they would gather in the woods for Mothers' Day. *Vergissmeinnicht* they called this flower in her mother tongue. Each year, on the eve of Mothers' Day, Liesl and her sister Hilde would slip away to the woods that covered hectares of their farm, to pick the blue flowers for their mother, and hide them in the barn until the morning; and every year their mother exclaimed afresh, in unfeigned pleasure at the 'surprise', as if she hadn't an inkling…

Liesl's favourite game of all was playing with her friend, the wind. She would run to meet it, then turn and let it pursue her. She would hold out her apron to catch it, but it always escaped. She would listen intently for the wind to tell her secrets, but it never warned her about the war… At this point, overwhelmed by images she could not block out, Frau Krüger's knees buckled and her eyes rolled back as she momentarily lost consciousness.

Slowly coming to her senses, she wondered in a confused way where she had been, and which part of the planet she had landed on. She became aware of arms enfolding her, and recognised them as belonging to her husband.

'It's over,' he said softly as she snuffled into his sweaty shirt front.

She started sobbing afresh. 'Trudi…'

'No, she's alive,' he said. 'Let's take her home now.'

Trudi lay on her side panting, covered in gore, froth on her bared teeth. Wrapping her in her apron, Frau Krüger lifted her up and cradled her to her chest.

'She'll live,' said Herr Krüger gently.

The goanna had vanished into the bracken. Neither of the Krügers noticed Helga, the speckled hen, surreptitiously emerge from her hiding place and follow them towards the farmhouse, red of comb and looking smug.

🌹 Frau Krüger's Rose

When Herr Krüger died, Frau Krüger felt she'd lost a large part of her life. Forty-seven shared years were torn in half, to be precise. Death is far worse than divorce, she reflected after the funeral. When people are divorced, they split the property, but when one half of a couple dies, that person takes half the shared memories with them, and the one left behind must work twice as hard to guard against time's petty thefts, so that the remaining memories don't follow the deceased to a place beyond retrieval. She sighed deeply, feeling the air enter then leave her chest. At least she was still breathing, but little more than that.

Herr Krüger's death had been sudden, and too soon, but no wonder, what with the war and the flight from the East, the refugee camps, worry about the children, migration, and sweated labour in the north Queensland canefields. That was just the prelude. It had enabled them to save enough to buy half-shares in a farm with another refugee family, compatriots of theirs – still in the tropics, in conditions unfamiliar to northern Europeans, near a small seaside resort noted for its friendly atmosphere and unpretentious charm. You could see the bay and part of the town from the farmhouse windows, which channelled the breeze from the sea, but only at the top of the slope where the house was. Down in the plantation it was always sweltering.

That was when the real work had begun. Three decades without respite, starting with a pawpaw crop that dropped from the trees almost at the point of harvest, blighted by some mysterious disease whose onset and progress had been invisible and thus unsuspected. The pawpaws were replaced by pineapples and tomatoes, and after seasons of backbreaking toil in the unrelenting heat, all had seemed to bode well for a bumper harvest, when an aftershock of the war that had thrust them into this other hemisphere devastated half the crop.

Mr Bill Crowe, who had sold them the farm, still owned the adjoining one. The farm bought by the Krügers and the Schmidts ran down the slope from the house to the arable land at the foot of a weathered, cone-shaped mountain whose apex had become worn down to a mound.

During the Second World War, the entire region had been swarming with Americans en route to the Pacific battlegrounds. They had cleared a rough road up the mountain and constructed a lookout at the very top. From there you could see for miles up and down the coast and out to the islands on the bay's eastern rim.

When the Americans were leaving, they needed to dispose of surplus ordnance, some of which consisted of drums of fuel, tar and unspecified chemicals. Bill Crowe, the Krügers' neighbour, had volunteered to take care of it, and so the drums had languished in his unkempt farmyard, corroding under rampant grass and weeds and encroaching lantana, along with assorted car bodies, tractor hulks and other scrap metal that Bill maintained might come in handy one day.

Despite the mistrust of Bill's cousin Norm towards the Krügers and the Schmidts, Bill remained on good terms with his new neighbours, whom he found industrious and decent. Norm, whose farm adjoined Bill's on the opposite side from the Krügers, remained sceptical, stroking his long sidewhiskers with a downward sweep of thumb and forefinger, his sad-sack face at its most lugubrious and disapproving.

The Krügers and Schmidts never missed the Sunday church service presided over by their Lutheran pastor. The remainder of the day was their only relief from the week's gruelling work. On Sunday evenings they lingered at the dining table in relaxed mood, savouring a bottle or two of wine and reminiscing about their adventures. Both families had a son and a daughter who avidly drank in their families' histories, trying to piece together some of the jagged fragments of their own lives.

One Sunday evening soon after they'd taken over the farm and were getting established, Mr Norman Crowe took it into his head to inspect his cousin's new neighbours, on the pretext of paying them a visit. Accordingly, at eight in the evening after his dinner, he knocked at the Krügers' door, having paused outside for long enough to register that the voices issuing from within were certainly not speaking English. In fact, they were not speaking, but singing, and that in a foreign tongue, which only served to intensify his suspicions that all was not as it should be. The only songs that could decently be sung on a Sunday were hymns. Methodist for preference, and certainly not in a foreign tongue! The strains that issued from behind and beneath the door most definitely bore no resemblance to Methodist hymns. Well then. This aberration lent authority to his knock.

Frau Krüger opened the door, her face flushed with surprise and a glass or two of wine. Recognising their near neighbour, she hastened to usher him to a chair and placed a wineglass in front of him, which, to Norm's horror, Herr Krüger hospitably proceeded to fill. The shock of it almost rendered the visitor speechless. Inventing a pretext, he made to go, saying he had to switch off the bore pump. He stumbled away in the dark as if inebriated – though he'd not touched a drop – stroking an imaginary beard between forefinger and thumb. The Krügers and the Schmidts thought Mr Crowe's behaviour a little odd and unsociable, but shrugged it off in the mood of conviviality that resumed as soon as he left.

The next day at breakfast, Mr Norman Crowe offered up a prayer for the sanctity of his household, and then announced, 'The Devil was dragging his tail around yonder den of iniquity last night.'

His children shrank in very fear at the name of sin personified.

Mr Bill Crowe, being of a more sanguine, lackadaisical disposition, did not share his cousin's misgivings, and two summers had gone by since the Devil had first been reported as dragging his tail around the Krüger-Schmidt farmhouse. It was a drowsy Sunday afternoon. The Krügers had attended church as usual, and had invited some friends for afternoon coffee. As they were about to partake, all hell broke loose. It sounded at first like a fireworks display, but that could never be. The Krügers and the Schmidts and their guests the Richters rushed outside in time to see jets of black smoke and spurts of flame issuing from Bill Crowe's backyard. The fuel drums had finally brewed their contents to an incendiary pitch, and a wildfire was unleashed that, by the end of the day, would scorch half the Krügers' soon-to-be-harvested pineapple and tomato crops. And in the process lend the force of prophecy to Mr Norman Crowe's appraisal of what he had witnessed at the Krüger-Schmidt household. 'Fire and brimstone!' he declared when the sea breeze carried the flames in that direction. His family's awe was gratifying.

*

'*Ach*, Herr Krüger!' Frau Krüger would sigh after his passing. 'What times we had! Why didn't you stay a while to relive them? We always shared everything – the terrible times and the laughs. We managed, Herr Krüger. Somehow we managed through thick and thin... But you squandered yourself, *mein Herr*, with all those free lessons you gave, year in, year out. French, German, so many pupils, and never once did you accept a *Pfennig*. All those lessons, here, there, and everywhere, after a day ploughing, planting pineapple suckers, chipping tomatoes, doing endless chores in the tropical sun. Our faces were burnt almost black by the time we called it a day and sold the second farm we bought, our own place. We had to build it up from scratch, remember? But our labours put Hannah and Klaus through boarding school and university, and even helped the grandchildren when they came along... No wonder your heart gave out, Herr Krüger, long before its time.

'The war took its toll. You were a prisoner of the British – though thank God for that, for I was captured by their Eastern allies. I was only sixteen, doing slave labour in Siberia. But we met and married after the war, and made a little world between us, out of the shards of a broken one. Our little world was like an egg, fragile, lovely and intact, new life inside it waiting to come out. And when the children were still infants, we escaped to West Berlin. Klaus and Hannah were both ill, in need of proper medicine. They were admitted to separate hospitals, two hours apart by foot. We walked the distance, hungry, freezing, just to save the fare... Herr Krüger, how our hearts were strong! We never let ourselves despair. We built a life with our bare hands, but now your heart has given out, and mine I think will not last long...'

Three years after Herr Krüger's death, Frau Krüger sold the house they'd bought for their retirement, with a swimming pool that failed to salvage either of their worn-out hearts. She proceeded to recreate her world in the image of previous versions, but on a smaller scale, in a cottage in a small retirement complex on the outskirts of a country township.

Before Herr Krüger died, they had returned to Germany on a visit, and been reunited with surviving relatives. Inevitably, it was not the world they'd known, so it was no great wrench to return to the home they had made and remade in a distant, different land.

Outside the cottage where she now lived alone, Frau Krüger planted a garden. Wherever she lived, she always planted things. Not far from her cottage, in a friend's yard in the township, grew a Norfolk Island pine tree Frau Krüger had grown from a seed. The seed had fallen from another Norfolk pine that had in turn germinated from a seed gathered in the main street of the seaside town near their first farm, the one they'd bought from Mr Bill Crowe at the foot of the mountain. The germination of living things, and the generations – of plants, of family – in this new homeland, mattered greatly to Frau Krüger.

So naturally she planted a small garden outside her cottage, and as always, even so late in life, she went about it methodically, taking time and pains, collecting as many different specimens of day-lilies as people would give her, building up an array of colours ranging from delicate shell pink through yolk-yellow to crimson. She planted geranium cuttings too, and a traditional red rose. For seven years she tended her little garden – which consisted of one large flower bed outside the door of her small, neat cottage – watering, weeding, pruning the rosebush.

Then her son and his wife, who lived close enough to visit her weekly, left for Europe on an extended working holiday, and she felt as if another petal of her life had been torn away. Frau Krüger had many friends, yet still she fretted for her son. Her daughter lived in another state, and she'd become reconciled to that. But lately she'd started having dizzy spells, and could not bend down to weed and plant and prune. She told the gardener at the retirement home that she could no longer take care of her plants, hoping he would come to the rescue.

One day, on returning from an excursion with other residents, Frau Krüger was aghast to find her lilies and geraniums gone. They had been uprooted and replaced by a six-inch-deep layer of wood chips, out of which poked, like a reproach, the bedraggled rosebush.

'I don't have time to run after people,' growled the gardener the next time their paths crossed. He couldn't look her in the eye. 'I've got too much other work to do.'

'But I could have given the lilies and geraniums to friends,' protested a voice in Frau Krüger's head. 'It took me seven years to collect all those colours…'

This time, several of the few remaining petals had been torn from what was left of Frau Krüger's life, the living, growing thing she had nurtured like a plant, a flowering species that could withstand many transplantings and still bloom joyously, despite adversity. Now even her poor rosebush had lost heart. One year ago, before they left, her son's wife had helped her prune it, as Frau Krüger's strength was already beginning to fail her.

'What happened to your garden, Frau Krüger?' asked her visitors. 'The flowers were so lovely!'

On the eve of the tenth anniversary of Herr Krüger's death, the so-called gardener had killed her garden.

'I cannot plant another one. I haven't got the strength,' Frau Krüger murmured to herself.

On the eve of the anniversary of Herr Krüger's death, Frau Krüger prepared to visit the cemetery. She would have no home-grown lilies to take this time. But the next morning it poured with rain. The surface would be too slippery for her to walk among the graves. All she could do was wave from the gate.

'*Guten Morgen*, Herr Krüger,' she called, and, hearing no answer, she sighed as she had many times since the day of his funeral, then blew a furtive kiss and said in a low voice, 'It rains too much. *Ich gehe jetzt*, Herr Krüger. *Auf Wiedersehen, mein lieber Herr, auf Wiedersehen…*'

'What has become of your garden, Frau Krüger?' *Ach*, but what had become of Frau Krüger? Her son and his wife had not yet noticed. They'd returned from abroad too preoccupied with their own concerns to realise the lilies were gone and the rose badly needed pruning.

People continued to visit, for wherever Frau Krüger went, she made friends. The friendships flourished like the plants that were so responsive to her nurturing presence. Many of the Krügers' earliest acquaintances from their farming days had become friends for life, and continued to phone and keep in touch. Some even travelled long distances from time to time, for the pleasure of Frau Krüger's company.

One day she received an unexpected visit from someone she'd almost forgotten, a pupil of Herr Krüger's from the old days. Now she had suddenly reappeared, grey-haired herself, but it didn't take Frau Krüger long to recognise her.

'Is it little Diane?' she said, blinking at the face in her doorway. 'I thought you have forgotten us. It's been so long…'

'I didn't know what had become of you, Frau Krüger,' explained the visitor. 'My father died, and my mother moved to another town, and then I lived abroad for half my life. The other day, quite by chance, I ran into a friend of Hannah's. She told me you were here…'

'Come in, come in,' Frau Krüger said. 'Tell me everything!'

The visitor had noticed the sad-looking rose poking out of the wood chips near the door, and recalled Frau Krüger's gift for making things grow. The wood chips looked somehow wrong. Inside, she noticed the half-finished embroidery Frau Krüger had laid on the sofa when she went to answer the doorbell. Blue flowers – forget-me-nots, *Vergissmeinnicht*, thought Diane, recalling reminiscences of Frau Krüger's childhood she had imbibed at their farmhouse long ago.

'I was so sorry to hear of Herr Krüger's passing,' Diane said as they sipped their coffee. 'I've brought you something in memory of his kindness to me and the other pupils.'

Excusing herself, she went out to her car. When Frau Krüger stood to follow her to the door, she came face to face with a rose tree in an urn. It was covered in claret-coloured rosettes of blossom.

'They promised me it was hardy,' said the bearer, breathless from the exertion of carrying it. 'They said it won't need much care – the people I bought it from…'

Frau Krüger felt a falling petal pause in mid-air and return to an invisible rose. She felt slightly dizzy. 'I must sit down,' she said.

The almost-stranger followed her inside, leaving the rose tree by the open door. 'When you feel better,' she said gently, passing Frau Krüger a glass of water, 'you can tell me where you'd like me to put Herr Krüger's rose…'

*

It seemed the petal that had paused in mid-air and returned to the stem of Frau Krüger's life marked the inception of a belated cycle of renewal. Being one of those whose green fingers are as naturally gifted in nurturing her own kind as they are with plants, Frau Krüger had touched many hearts in her passage through life, one of whom lived close by, in another cottage in the same precinct: a woman as fiercely independent as she was loyal.

When Diane returned some weeks later, the wood chips and the black polythene sheeting they had rested on, not allowing the soil to breathe and stifling all growth, had been banished, and jubilant shoots and sprouts and clusters of green adorned the garden bed. A beaming Frau Krüger, her spirits restored, greeted Diane at the door.

'I see you've got your garden back,' said Diane.

Frau Krüger regarded her visitor with beatific eyes. 'This garden is the gift of my dear friend Violet,' she said. 'This is what I see when I look at its leaves and buds: the hands of a beloved friend reaching out to me… This is how life is, *nicht wahr?* It just waits for a kind word, a caring touch, a little water, a little sun, and it fills our hands with roses, and perfumes the air with their breath…'

Softly, as if to herself, she added, '*Das reicht mir im Leben… Ja…*'

For me this is enough.

Billy Hunter

Billy Hunter sat in the tin and timber structure that served as office and living quarters at the whistle-stop rail station, watching the air darken above the deserted tracks. His chair by the door faced the dusty slab of platform. Cradled in one elbow and resting across his knees like a musical instrument was a .22 rifle – his new friend. He had the aspect of a person waiting for something, or someone.

Although it was only eight weeks since he'd acquired Betsy, as he called the rifle, such is the condition of infatuation that it tends to obliterate memories of anything that preceded it. Billy's life as the sole attendant of this hellhole at the edge of the world had undergone a transformation since he'd got his gun.

He could of course remember how it had been before that. Lonely. Terrifying. Spooky. Insane. Months and months of feeling his mind coming adrift. The brigalow scrub was worse than a prison. If you were in jail at least your fate was shared by others. Here there were no fellow-sufferers. And outside the prison walls you knew there was some form of civilisation: shops, houses, families – people! What was there here? A dirt road dissolving in scrub, a railway track outside the door, trains that seldom stopped, and brigalow. A sea of it.

Billy knew some of the people submerged in that sea. That is, he knew who they were, he'd sometimes eavesdropped on their party line, a local telephone network that invited breach of privacy. He sometimes tapped their grapevine, just to scratch the itch of isolation.

So he knew that one of the daughters of a prominent grazier was spending time rolling in the hay with the district horse-breaker. He guessed she must have been lonely too. He knew of land deals being cut, so that the big fish could get bigger by swallowing the few remaining small fry. Billy also knew who had a secret drinking problem, and who was cheating on whom. This knowledge had been acquired gradually, snippet by snippet, over many months. You had to learn how to read between the lines, and put two and two together. It was a bit like doing a crossword or a jigsaw, and he knew about those too. But there are only so many crosswords and jigsaws a person can do before it all starts to gyrate in your head and add to the general chaos.

Billy, with a lopsided grin, would fantasise from time to time that there were quite a few potential targets, invisible out there in the scrub, people he could hold to ransom if he so desired. Just a little blackmail note here and there. They'd never suspect him, because while he knew some of them by sight from the occasional goods deliveries to the siding, none of them ever so much as looked at him. 'Boy,' they would call him. Like a dog. 'Here, boy, give us a hand to load this fencing wire, would you?'

No thanks, no reward, no word of acknowledgement that this was a fellow human being. Once in a while, perhaps an impersonal 'Good lad!' Of course, the sort of men who passed through the siding were impressed by brawn, and it had always been a source of secret heartache to Billy that his own physique was closer to scrawn – what kindlier souls, such as his Aunt Sally, might refer to as 'wiry'. But more like a jockey than a lumberjack, in fact.

No, blackmail was too good for the likes of that lot!

It was getting on for a year since he'd been posted to this hole. 'Gotta do the hard yards before you can go for a cushy job!' they'd told him cheerfully. Nobody had mentioned how long it might take for the tide to turn. Oh, sure, he got four days off every fortnight – a day's train ride to the city, a taste of his mum's cooking, a couple of hot showers, clean sheets and a bed you could actually rest in, then it was load up the clean socks and jocks and climb on the train for the back of beyond, where the radio reception was up to shit, and he'd jump at the sound of his own voice.

He'd never been what you'd call a great reader, but reading did help to pass the time, that was for sure. A stack of fly-specked cheap paperbacks climbed the wall in one corner, but it was like the jigsaws and crosswords. There were only so many words you could swallow without getting indigestion. He'd worked his way through whodunnits, Westerns – Zane Grey and Louis L'Amour, a string of repetitive scenarios – and lingered over Cormac McCarthy's *Blood Meridian: Or, the Evening Redness in the West*. Now that was a story he'd not forget! He'd really identified with the hero. The characters and their wild lives had made him forget he was stuck in this dump. They'd taken him along for the ride. Their world was also a desolate, desperate place, but at least things happened there.

Since he'd bought Betsy, his trusty rifle, what difference had this made? For a start, it made him feel different. As if he could be the one in control, for a change. Otherwise, what was his life? He was stuck in the middle of nowhere, where nobody even spared him a thought. There had to be someone in attendance here to set the points to the siding, even though only two trains a day, one coming north, one going south, passed through the station, seldom stopping for passengers or goods.

In fact, although he'd loved trains as a child, he'd been watching them go past for so long that now they made him sick. He resented the way the drivers grinned and waved from the locomotive, or didn't grin and wave, acknowledging the existence of the siding only with a piercing whistle, not even bothering to slacken pace as they sped on their way. They were mobile, he was not.

But somehow he felt different with the gun in his hands. He would grin to himself, imagining the look on the face of an engine-driver approaching the platform and suddenly noticing that he was in Billy's rifle sights. Of course, he wouldn't be such a fool as to try a joke like that, but even imagining it was good for a laugh.

He didn't fancy killing animals either, except for snakes. He'd rather shoot at fence posts, or tin cans on a box. He didn't plan to kill anything really. He just felt that the gun sort of empowered him. Gave him some clout. Not that anyone would notice, but it was a good feeling just the same.

*

It was a Saturday, eight weeks after he'd taken possession of Betsy, and halfway through Billy's usual ten-day stint in Woop Woop. He'd had a couple of cans of beer, which was illegal for someone on duty. A rare reward for helping a bloke load some freight. Pity to let it get hot. It was six hours before the next train was due through, so he decided to cut across to the highway, two hours' walk away, to break the monotony. He knew the short-cut, he'd done it a few times before, now that he had Betsy for protection. Against regulations, naturally, which required him to be at his post at all times, just in case. But who would notice? His relief on his four days off used to say he couldn't have stuck it. Even four days and nights in the bush gave him the creeps, and he couldn't wait to escape.

Billy headed off on a bridle path through the scrub, made when the siding had functioned as a mail exchange. He fired into the air a couple of times, just for the hell of it, sending a few crows into momentary panic.

He was in a strange mood as he approached the road, light-headed, a trifle tipsy at this break in routine, as if he could just keep going and never return to that place of incarceration, where he might as well wear a ball and chain.

He noticed some smoke rising at the old stockyards to one side of the highway, and decided on a stealthy approach, partly for the fun of surprising whoever was there, and partly in case it was someone who'd know he was playing hookey. Not that he cared right now. It might be the best favour he'd ever done himself, if he got himself sacked.

Billy soon realised that it was nobody local. The camper van had Tasmanian registration. Circling round to get a better view, he noticed an elderly couple sitting on folding chairs near a campfire, the woman holding a steaming mug, the man poring over a map on his knees.

Billy watched them with curiosity, envious of their mobility. Here today, gone tomorrow. Someone to talk to, new things to see, while only a few miles away across country he lived as if on another planet.

Just fooling around, he lifted his rifle, training the sights on the elderly man. As if she sensed something, the woman swung round abruptly in her chair. In a nervous reflex, Billy squeezed the trigger, heard the shot, and then a cry from the man crumpled over the map, before he turned and ran.

His breath was ragged, his mind numb as he reached the siding in record time. Cradling Betsy in one elbow, Billy took up his post on a chair by the open door, as the dark came down on the scrub and the rails still hot from the sun began to contract.

The Curlew's Cry

After my marriage to Gerald came to an abrupt end, I signed on as a volunteer with a local wildlife rescue organisation. I suppose there was a connection between the two events, in that helping other creatures in distress was a step in restoring a sense of purpose and empowerment to my life, which for too long had orbited around Gerald's career. As it turned out, he'd actually been leading a double life for years, under the guise of working extended hours in his managerial capacity. So much for wifely devotion!

It was around midnight on a Saturday that I received my fourth call-out for the evening – from a security guard at a bay-side premises, who had found a curlew entangled in fishing line with the hook still attached. The bird was emaciated. Its keel bone protruded visibly beneath its breast feathers and it weighed next to nothing in my hands. The ambulance driver, experienced in such cases, suggested contacting a local family that specialised in the rescue and care of injured birds, and so it was that I met the three 'bird women', who spanned three generations of one family – grandmother, mother, daughter. Their lives had become intertwined with the lives of birds, a trajectory that set them apart from other people I knew.

When I arrived with the bird in the ambulance, I was met by the second of the women, who was soon joined by her mother and daughter. They told me they'd been out in their boat that afternoon, going to the rescue of pelicans which had, like the curlew, become entangled in fishing lines and hooks. There were injured birds in padded cages in various rooms of the large house, and the women kept their voices low, so as not to alarm their avian patients.

The two younger women briefly discussed what would be best for the curlew, which regarded them with its large, light-shy eyes but did not flinch or struggle. They told me the best technique for removing the fishing line was not to unwind it, as it had cut into the skin on one leg, exposing the tendon and bone, but to snip the line into sections with surgical scissors before removing it, which they deftly proceeded to do.

As they removed the last bit of line, the bird uttered a low cry, seemingly not of pain, but perhaps of acknowledgement, or relief. The women then applied Manuka honey to the injured leg, followed by medicated gel and dressings. They slipped a dose of antibiotic, calculated in accordance with the bird's weight, into its beak, placed it in a cage with a rolled towel supporting its head and neck so that the medicine wouldn't be regurgitated, and told me they thought the curlew stood a chance of survival, while voicing concern at its emaciated state.

I left about an hour after midnight. My encounter with the women, their house that sheltered injured birds – a nest woven from human care and carefully accumulated strands of bird lore – and the work they did, with no external support, yet with such skill and commitment, had greatly impressed me and given me food for thought. How could it be that in some families the generations meshed without friction, interweaving their inner resources to generate healing energies and a spirit of reciprocal support; whereas in others, such as mine, there were painful rifts and unravellings running through several generations, for which there appeared to be no remedy? Even to speak of the problem was to exacerbate it.

As I was driven home in the ambulance, I recalled a scene from the previous summer. Early one evening, I'd been driving home through quiet suburban avenues when something reared into view in the beam of the headlights, causing me to brake in alarm and pull over to the kerb. Turning off the ignition, I got out, and was confronted by two tall, spectral-looking birds, their wings extended to full span, emitting harsh, fricative, hissing sounds to warn me off. Their pinions were the ghostly fawn of certain moths, marked on the underside, which was now exposed, by white ovals and striations. It took me a moment to realise that these were curlews. Drawn to their full height with phalanges at full stretch, they were regal, imposing, quite unlike the darting, torpedo-shaped creatures of the shadows I had often glimpsed on my morning walks along the foreshore near my home.

I soon understood the reason for this unequal stand-off. The parent birds were shepherding two chicks across the road, from the golf links on one side to the park on the other. They had forced me to stop the car, but what might have happened if it had been a different driver, travelling faster? I watched the chicks – covered in white down with dark dorsal stripes, so small and frail they must have been newly hatched – struggle to surmount the kerb, their cheeping, whistling cries signalling distress. Agitated, the parent birds shuttled between their hatchlings, protective, encouraging, but unable to assist the transition from asphalt to park. Then one chick, with an almighty effort, scrambled up onto the grass, whereas its sibling was rapidly tiring, running along the gutter parallel to the kerb, making ineffectual lunges in an attempt to overcome the obstacle. I looked on helplessly, my heart in my mouth.

Fortuitously, the stranded chick reached a driveway where there was no kerb. The parents and I were palpably relieved when it tottered onto the grass. With urgent shepherding sounds I'd never before heard, the adult curlews escorted their young swiftly to the shadow cast by a tree, where they seemed to melt into the dappled pattern projected by moonlight through leaves. I lingered a few moments longer, reflecting on what I had witnessed. No match for a vehicle, the adult curlews were nonetheless fearsome, dauntless in their efforts to ensure safe passage for their offspring.

As I resumed my homeward journey, another scene came to mind, prompted by the behaviour of the curlew parents. Near the front gate of the farm where I'd grown up with my siblings was a massive old bluegum. We'd waited beneath its lofty branches every morning for the rural school bus. One day, as part of a council plan to widen the dirt access road, a bulldozer had arrived to make an assault on the tree.

Alerted by the grunting, roaring, tearing sounds the dozer emitted, our mother had rushed down the track to the road and flung herself in front of the mechanical brute, arms raised in the same gesture as that of the parent curlews. In the end, thanks solely to our mother's resistance, the tree had been spared.

Was bravery instinctive or a conscious act? Would it make it any less admirable if it were involuntary?

*

At about four a.m., I woke in my house by the bay to the wailing of curlews on the foreshore, and remembered the bird I'd delivered to safety a few hours before, now lying in a soft, warm nest in a darkened house, registering the energies and frequencies transmitted by the other avian and human occupants, and, I hoped, feeling safe and comfortable. One of the women had told me that birds responded quickly to antibiotics, but the first few hours were crucial, as they could succumb to shock.

My mind reached out to the bird, poised on the limen between life and death. Some part of me had attached itself to the stricken curlew's fate. I needed to believe this bird would survive and rejoin her family group on the foreshore, darting along the sand beneath the casuarinas in swift glissades so fluid that she melded into moonlight. Immobile in the light of day, camouflaged by the tawny surroundings of bark, or sand, or grass, curlew plumage was subtly marked to resemble shadow streaked with muted light, the body elegantly tapered on stilt-like legs, with a large cranium on the slender neck and extraordinary, unbirdlike eyes that seemed to scan your soul.

Wary of contact with humans, curlews were nonetheless close observers of people. Even by day, resting in the shade of melaleucas, they would watch you without your being aware of them. It always startled me to suddenly realise they were there, and to see those golden irises and dilated pupils trained on me. I thought of them as spirit birds, totems of my own rural clan, slipping like phantoms through the ether between the earthly and unearthly; curdling the blood at night with their wailing redolent of lamentation, desolation. Harbingers of the unknowable, the wild and lonely criers of my childhood, they seemed to give voice to something I could sense but had no words for. Something to do with life's totality; its devastating intensity, its uncompromising brevity, the plangency of unassuageable longing.

I so hoped the bird's leg would heal. Her wings were unharmed, and her spirit was perhaps at that moment running beside the shallow tide that lapped in from the bay. I recalled again the low cry the bird had uttered as the women finished disentangling her. It seemed to be a cry of relief at her deliverance at the hands of another species. At an instinctive, personal level, this was how I perceived the sound. Not that I could ever really know.

I reflected again on the women's practical compassion, their willingness to sacrifice their own comfort and rest to go to the assistance of creatures in distress. The women seemed blessed in their sense of purpose. The harmonious give and take they unconsciously practised in their work was something I'd longed for in my own life, in my family, my marriage… I wished I could take my siblings, my estranged husband, to the house that had been transformed into a sanctuary for injured birds, and show them: 'See, this is a place of healing. Couldn't we learn to change our ways, lose the impulse to inflict hurt, and regain a sense of our innate innocence? Couldn't we try to cultivate the grace of forbearance, compassion…?'

But recovery was not to be. The nightwatchman had found the bird too late. Infection had entered the curlew's bones, and no antibiotic could save it. The cries I'd heard along the shore were keening. The next night I'd set out again to play my part in rescuing the hurt, the trapped, and creatures threatened by disease. That work would not wait.

The mantle of recovery was full of holes and knots, broken and snagged threads that had become snarled. This mantle was difficult to weave, and sometimes heart-rending, but the work of mending must go on, if life was to have wholeness and coherence. Destruction was a swift, careless, often wanton reflex, whereas healing was slow, and required great patience. Tending hurt creatures was arduous, but for the sake of that cryptic plumage, those golden eyes, the cries that carried from the shore the note of all still free and wild, I knew I'd sacrifice my sleep, my time, my energy; keep hope alive. I knew I needed this as much as the creatures I helped to rescue. To ease the Earth's ache for an instant – was that too much to ask?

For some of the birds that were brought to the women's sanctuary, it was an ending, but at least they did not die alone, afraid and in pain. For others, random casualties of human carelessness, the care they received in the women's house and hands was a new beginning.

Hovering Over My Life

In retrospect, I'd have to say it started with the heart. My heart, which inexplicably, three decades into the twenty-first century, defied the advance-warning systems of modern medical technology and defaulted in its duties. Malfunctioning valves, they said, which could be rectified by surgery involving the transplanting of valves from a pig's heart.

Now, I happen to know there are far more sophisticated technologies available, ranging from synthetic valves to synthetic hearts. As assistant to the director of the Department of Innovation (who happens to be my current partner), I am well aware of consumer choices. I'm also aware of the advances achieved with the latest generation of superswine, whose organs have been genetically modified to attain the highest possible degree of compatibility with human tissue without the stigma attached to using human clones as organ donors, while also sidestepping issues surrounding the controversial illicit traffic in human organs, which has reached epic proportions in the last three decades. So I duly signed the document consenting to a procedure whereby I would become the recipient of part of the heart of a pig.

While I had no qualms about the competency of my medical team, what I hadn't bargained for was the way the past was about to catch up with me on levels other than the physical. As I approached my fiftieth birthday in the year 2031, I was unaware that early personal experience from which I'd long since distanced myself had in fact turned into a crocodile biding its time, and was now about to take me by the throat and threaten to drag me under. I, meanwhile, had spent three decades believing life is a skill set and that's all there is to it.

Lulled by the latest drugs patented by our own department, I was indulging in some gratifying post-surgical flashbacks about how far we've come since the close of that confused, bulimic century, the twentieth. Thanks largely to our department, unprecedented innovation has occurred in almost every aspect of daily life. The citizens of the twentieth century had seemingly only dimly perceived that their personal, social and political problems were, above all, management issues. Now, thanks to some inspired directives and social programming initiatives, the mess and excess of the twentieth century are a thing of the past. Those of us whose energies and influence drove this quantum leap prefer not to look back, but with time on my hands to reflect, I'm afraid I succumbed to temptation.

For instance, since the annual review criterion has been extended to personal life, what used to be termed 'relationships' have been redesignated as contracts. This annual option (indeed, obligation) of renewing one's partnership contract (analogous to renewing one's vehicle registration) has tidied up the domestic fallout considerably. Admittedly, partnerships involving children presented some teething problems, but as more and more parents take advantage of the full range of genetic options, it becomes easier to implement reform.

Although I have mentioned my imminent fiftieth birthday, we've dispensed with the cloying sentiment associated with birthdays since the inception of a programme devised by myself and an elite planning team for social strategies – the 'use-by date' scheme for senior citizens – whereby one's tenure on life beyond the age of seventy-five is subject to annual review, and redundancy notices are issued to those who have little or nothing further to contribute, in terms of productivity, to this progressive society. Those deemed unsustainable in accordance with our rigorous criteria are then put on notice to enter a programme to prepare them for voluntary euthanasia, thereby rationalising and legitimising what was already tacit though clandestine practice.

It gives me a sense of personal accomplishment to be able to report that birth, partnership, parenthood and death are now moderated as never before, which has done much to eradicate the waste and economic fallout of a few decades ago. (As a corollary, we have all but eliminated the need for charity and the role of charities.) Indeed, I am proud of the fact that my own mother was one of the first volunteers in the euthanasia pilot scheme, setting an example, as she said, for my sake. And it was at that point in my mental review that my thoughts spun off at a tangent.

Without warning, I seemed to sense my mother's presence at my hospital bedside, although the night light illumined only an empty chair. It was as if a pressure valve had been released, and all the dross of the past had come gushing out. Lacerating reminders of incidents that had discoloured my childhood, long since resolutely expunged from memory, resurfaced to taunt me, along with golden, carefree moments, their lustre enhanced by the irrevocable nature of such things.

As if hovering over my own life, I was simultaneously seeing it in its entirety and in precise, dissociated detail. I saw myself as a small boy cuddling my cat in our overgrown garden, and running with my friends in the park beside the river. I saw myself in my room, surrounded by Lego blocks and books and model dinosaurs, all laid out with taxonomic precision, my untidy mother somewhere in the offing, poring over her self-help books or writing interminable letters in support of prisoners of conscience, while my absentminded father barricaded himself in his study and immersed himself in research into lost civilisations. I was at the fulcrum of their seesaw, although the analogy is hardly apt, as the rhythm of our household was erratic at best.

An all but forgotten interlude swam into focus, from when I was aged about nine. At that time, all my weekends were spent in the company of Timothy. We had been inseparable since kindergarten days, in fact, and our weekends alternated between my house and Tim's or, more frequently, Tim's grandmother's. She indulged us equally. We called her red-brick home the Gingerbread House, and she was like a fairy godmother who knew exactly what creature comforts boys needed in order to feel blissfully content.

Tim's grandma never scolded us, but then we seldom gave her cause. She cooked appetising, hearty meals with lots of rich puddings, and baked cakes and biscuits for snacks. There were games and videos

I didn't have at home and a house full of familial objects that appealed to my curiosity. There were soft, fragrant beds and cosy armchairs, quite unlike the Spartan conditions at my home, and Tim's doting grandma was lavish with hugs and endearments. It's usually only in fairy tales that you meet people like her, but she was as real as could be. We liked staying with her so much that we made up stories about being orphans so that we could live at the gingerbread house all the time. We even cast spells. Tim was good at that. He had an audacious imagination.

Accordingly, over several weekends we helped ourselves to some of my mother's jewellery – a silver butterfly brooch with a naked woman's body, probably Art Nouveau as I realise now – and a choker made of black mother-of-pearl. We also found a photo of her when she was younger. One Saturday, while she was doing the grocery shopping, we buried these objects, with spells and incantations, under a big tree in the far corner of the back yard. I remember feeling rather relieved when the spell didn't take effect. Somehow the project lost impetus, abandoned in favour of other games.

I could not bring myself to zero in on the events that abruptly terminated what seems, in retrospect, an idyllic early childhood. To my acute dismay, images of brutal loss of innocence, frozen like laboratory slides, still carried enough charge to induce a sense of utter disempowerment. My parents should have recognised the predator for what he was, yet neither before nor after did they notice anything untoward. By the time I broke the news to them, more to make them aware of their own shortcomings than because it could make any difference to me, it was too late to repair the damage. They had lost me. We had lost each other. The hollow myth of family had become anathema to me.

Perhaps it is my misfortune to be born into a transitional generation, although every generation is in some sense transitional, and perceives itself as such. My mother used to say it was her generation that broke the ice, by igniting the social and sexual revolution of the 1960s and 70s. I cannot forget how the children of that revolution – myself and my peers – would cringe at any reminder of the outmoded quaintness and naïveté of my mother's generation, with their folk songs and flowers and motley clothes, hallucinogenic experimentation, ashrams and meditation; their irresponsible couplings and inept parenting: free spirits who left us to pick up the tab for their self-indulgence – the mess we inherited, and had to develop the tools to deal with.

It would be unthinkable for my partner and me to go back to those days, even if that were possible. I would not want to belong to that generation of dinosaurs trailing 'rags and feathers from Salvation Army counters'. Yet one sometimes tires of the impersonality of the new model of partnership: an annual contract, renewable subject to mutual negotiation. No real strings and no real attachment; an efficient way to manage one's daily life, tidy as a tenancy agreement. An undeniable advance on the messiness of late twentieth-century 'relationships', as they were called. Even so, there are times when one's personal life seems too tame, too standardised.

My mother did not in fact embrace the flower-child syndrome, living for today with no thought of tomorrow and no accountability. She tended more to the social conscience faction, was a passionate advocate of education as a means to equity, active in the women's movement, but there was nevertheless a whiff of incense in her aura, and she never did get the hang of anything that smacked of the corporate. Her drug was travel, and I was part of the baggage that accompanied her, though to give her her due, she perceived educational benefits in every border crossing that I for the life of me could not discern.

That night in the hospital, as I began to drift into a cosy, medicated fog, I heard my mother's voice at my bedside.

'Larry,' she was saying, 'please don't ever lose your special vision of what life can be. I remember what a kind, caring, compassionate boy you were, always with a desire to help those who have less. Don't lose your way. Ambition is all very well in its place, but don't forget to be kind. Practical acts of kindness – that's what the world needs more of...'

(In 2031 we don't use that word – kindness – any more. It has slipped out of usage as an inadequate, vague, ineffectual term. Along with words like conscience and humanism, it eludes precise definition and impedes efficiency.)

A silence ensued, when I sensed she was still at my bedside, watching me, though I couldn't see her.

'Larry, I'm sorry you had to put up with my messy relation-ships, my life as a haphazard work in progress. You were so dear to me, the one pure thing: a glimpse of perfection in a world flawed by human frailty. I doubt I communicated that clearly enough, or often enough... But you know why I've come, don't you? I've come to ask your forgiveness. You know what for. You were under my protection, and I failed to notice the threat to you – the predator, watching and waiting his chance. I was not even aware of his existence, and I've never forgiven myself for that. Yet I'm sad that you carry the weight in your soul that is the inability to forgive. Although you may never be able to forgive the predator – just as I cannot – why can you not find it in your heart to forgive me for what I failed to sense or foresee?'

I wanted to laugh bitterly, to cry. Involuntary memories of my family life, my uncool, chronically uncoordinated mother, had been the most imperfect thing in a world I'd tried to make as streamlined, as perfect as possible. Given that I was not on good terms with my past, remembering her meant reliving events over which I'd had no control; feelings that threatened to swamp me, take me down to some murky, sublimated place where I never again wanted to be. It meant remembering words that had no place in my twenty-first-century portfolio: words like 'relationships', 'emotions', 'forgive', 'soul', 'psyche', 'charity', 'compassion', 'empathy' – and, most recondite of all, 'kindness'. These were active agents in my mother's vocabulary that had become superfluous to mine, the unclaimed baggage of a chaotic century. As architects of social change we have, moreover, well and truly deconstructed 'love'.

The most bizarre image of the encounter filled the silence that followed her flow of speech. I saw myself as an infant, bathed in the light of a love I'd long forgotten in the transition to a life lived under the terms of various contracts. As that unsuspected casualty, my heart, went into an agonising spasm, I heard her saying 'Good night, Larry, sweet dreams', the way she used to, and I fancied I felt her breath on my skin as her lips brushed my cheek. Then the light went out.

For the first and only time, I'd seen my life whole, imperfect and painful, but mine, my own, the gift of my loving, imperfect, conscience-stricken mother.

Since my recovery, I have not been able to re-enter a present that excludes the past, because when I was hovering over my life, I saw the past alive in the present, in effect ever-present, whether acknowledged or not. And her words haunt me. Kindness…what if she was right, and kindness was the key to it all? The notion seemed too nebulous, until I recalled Tim's grandma, her unfailing kindness to us boys. When we deleted this word from our language, did we extinguish the idea, the deed?

While my heart was intact, I was not troubled by notions of interpretation. Every aspect of living was unambiguously defined in accordance with our ingenious social policy. This relieved the populace of the burden and confusion that ensues when each person has to think for him or her self.

Now, a change of valve has seemingly coincided with, or perhaps caused, a change of heart. A change of values. Paradoxically, since receiving part of the heart of a pig, I've begun to feel more human, as they used to say: that is, less mechanical in the way I think and act. I am no longer the person I believed myself to be, or to have become, yet I feel more myself – more at home with myself. It's easier for me to feel compassion, but at the same time harder to bear the pain of empathy. There occurred at some point the sudden, troubling realisation that I no longer want to be a bureaucrat. I just want to be a loving, caring human being – a practitioner of kindness.

Acknowledgements

'Reading Rilke' and 'Little Black Dress' (as 'Aunt Matilda's Party Dress') were published in the Black Inc anthologies *Best Australian Stories 2004* and *2005* respectively, edited by Frank Moorhouse. 'Aunt Matilda's Party Dress' was also broadcast on ABC Radio National's *Sunday Story*. 'Billy Hunter' was the winner of the Open section, Bauhinia Short Story Award 2007 and was published in *Idiom 23*. Other stories, including 'The Gamblers', 'Fool's Gold', 'The Girl and the Tiger', 'Death by Water' ('The Agency of Water') and 'Poor Blighter' have been commended or highly commended in various competitions. 'Voices in the Wind' was published in the sesquicentennial anthology *Hibiscus and Ti-Tree: Women in Queensland*, edited by Carole Ferrier and Deborah Jordan (St Lucia, Hecate Press, 2009). 'Praise Be' ('The Agency of Love') was the winner, Pacific region, in the 2010 Commonwealth Short Story Competition. 'The Agency of Water' was published in *Mascara Literary Review*, Issue 11, June 2012. 'No Such Address' appeared in *Transnational Literature*, Volume 5, Issue 2, May 2013. The scenario of 'The Zeigarnik Effect' is based in part on impressions and recollections of a Márta Mészáros film, *The Heiresses* (1980). 'The Tale of the Girl and the Tiger' was inspired by Sergei Bodrov senior's film *Bear's Kiss* (2002).

The lines quoted as an epigraph on page 6 are from the author's poem sequence 'Monemvasia', in *Eros in Landscape* (Milton, Jacaranda Press, 1989). The quotation from *The Rubaiyat* of Omar Khayyam on page 43 is from the Fitzgerald translation.

Special thanks must go to certain members of the medical profession, particularly Professor Owen Ung, Dr Alison Hadley, Dr Michelle Grogan, Dr Graham Radford-Smith, Hildegard Reul-Hirche and their colleagues at RBWH, without whose timely and decisive intervention there would have been no more stories. My thanks also to Dr Renu Kumar.

There are many other people to whom my gratitude is due. Foremost among them are Evie and Sidney; my daughter Larisa; my sisters Alice and Nelia; and my friends and well-wishers Betty Beath, Vera Black, Gillian Bouras, Lorraine Brandle, Victor Comino, Natalie Devine, Calliope Fardoulys, Svyetlana Hadgraft, Shahimah Idris, Joan Keating, Janet Lovery, Lazaros Mavromatis, Nerida O'Hare, Elisa Piliaris, Rosalba Ribecco, Donna Schabe, Paul Sherman, Kyria Elli Tepelena, Katie Tregear, and Rex and Tom Tripcony, whose energy, support and unfailing kindness have been sustaining on many levels.

Zbyn k Černík and Marcia McMenamin read the manuscript and offered helpful comments. I am indebted too to Dr Gay Lynch (Flinders University) for a timely wake-up call. Stuart O'Hare provided advice on some technical matters.

A Hawthornden Fellowship at the Hawthornden International Retreat for Writers (Scotland) provided the time and tranquillity for revision and editing and also an opportunity to road test some of the stories on fellow writers, so I would like to express my appreciation for the generous and gracious patronage extended to me as a guest of Hawthornden Castle.

Also at Hawthornden, my heartfelt thanks to Hamish Robinson.

Robyn Sheahan-Bright has offered invaluable advice on editorial matters, for which I am immensely grateful, while Stephen Matthews has once again assumed the role of ideal reader and publisher, for which no words of gratitude can suffice. *Pro captor lectoris habent sua fata libelli*. May the work prove worthy.

www.ingramcontent.com/pod-product-compliance
Lightning Source LLC
Chambersburg PA
CBHW030910080526
44589CB00010B/235